THE LONDON THEATRE GUIDE

GUIDE

Richard Andrews

The London Theatre Guide

Written by Richard Andrews
Cover photographs:
(top) Shakespeare's Globe by Andrea Pistolesi
(bottom) Grand Duo by Mark Royce
(back)by Derek Kendall © English Heritage
Edited by Abigail Willis
Seating Plans designed by Lesley Gilmour
Design by Metro

Published in 2002 by
Metro Publications
PO Box 6336
London
N1 6PY

Printed and bound in Spain by Imago

© 2002 Richard Andrews

British Library Cataloguing in Publication Data.
A catalogue record for this book is available from the British Library.

ISBN 1 902910 08 7

Open Air, Regents Park

CONTENTS

ACKNOWLEDGMENTS

Thanks go to English Heritage for all the photographs they have provided to use within this book. In particular we want to thank Derek Kendall whose keen eye has created many beautiful photographs and June Warrington for her generosity and patience. Gareth at Epo Online was also a great help to us and unearthed many splendid pictures at short notice. We are also grateful to all the theatre staff who have provided information at short notice to make sure that this book is as accurate as possible. Lastly, Abigail Willis deserves special thanks for her efforts in editing this book.

SAFETY CURTAIN

Garrick Theatre

INTRODUCTION

The aim of this book is to provide a complete guide for anyone visiting a London Theatre - and in the year 2001 that was almost 12 million theatregoers. On a practical level, it brings together all the essentials, including seating plans and detailed information on the facilities of the West End theatres, plus box office numbers, as well as tips on how to get cheap (or even free) seats. Those who enjoy the history and stories of London's theatres will also find plenty to interest them. For example, there is the tale of actor William Terris, who was murdered by fellow thespian Richard Archer in 1897 outside the Adelphi, and whose ghost is said to roam the still gas lit alleyways surrounding the theatre to this day. The idiosyncratic customs and language of the theatre have not been neglected either. Here's your chance to find out why actors are called 'thespians', what 'The Half' is, and why it is unlucky to mention the actual name of 'The Scottish Play'.

I have also included in depth information about the architecture of West End theatres, from the grand design of Benjamin Wyatt's Theatre Royal Drury Lane, London's oldest, and arguably the world's greatest theatre, to the modern steel and glass of the new Sadler's Wells. You can even find out how to get involved in theatre by becoming an Angel. Many of the photographs that accompany the text are provided by English Heritage and wonderfully illustrate the grandeur and architectural details to be found in the Capital's theatres. I hope you enjoy the book as much as I have enjoyed writing it, but above all, I hope that it encourages you to visit London's theatres, and experience the magic of live performance for yourselves.

Richard Andrews
2002

OVERTURE - THE HISTORY

Duchess Theatre

Facts & Figures

Record Breakers

The longest running play is Agatha Christie's *The Mousetrap* which opened at the Ambassadors on 25th November 1952, transferring to the St Martin's next door on 25th March 1974 where it continues to break records. Although originally some actors remained in it for long periods – the record is held by Nancy Seabrook who was an understudy for 16 years – the cast now changes annually.

London's longest running comedy is *No Sex Please We're British*, by Anthony Marriott and Alistair Foot which opened at the Strand on 3rd June 1971, transferring to the Garrick in 1982 and again to the Duchess in 1986 where its record breaking run ended on 5th September 1987.

Andrew Lloyd Webber's *Cats*, takes the prize for longest running musical; it opened at the New London Theatre on 11th May 1981 and closed exactly 21 years later on 11th May 2002.

The world's first musical is claimed by some to be John Gay's *The Beggar's Opera* produced in 1728 by actor manager John Rich at Lincoln's Inn Fields theatre. It was so successful that it became renowned for "having made Gay rich and Rich gay". Folk tunes of the day were interpolated in the story of a notorious criminal, MacHeath, satirising the corruption of politicians and officials. Gay's next work *Polly* (which continued the story) was banned, becoming the first play to be subject to censorship by the Lord Chamberlain.

Britain's first pantomime was staged by John Rich at Lincoln's Inn Fields in 1716, when he played Harlequin in an adaptation of an Italian comic ballet. He continued to present it each Christmas until 1760. The word pantomime was first used to describe a performance at Drury Lane in 1717.

The first British revue was *Under The Clock,* produced in 1893 by Seymour Hicks and Charles Brookfield.

The first public playhouse in Britain was The Theatre, constructed outside the city wall to the north in Shoreditch in 1576, built and managed by the actor James Burbage.

The first British star actor was his son Richard Burbage, the actor manager of the Globe, who created most of the leading roles in Shakespeare's plays.

The first actor to be knighted was Henry Irving in 1895, and the first to receive a peerage was Laurence Olivier in 1970.

Females did not appear on stage until theatres reopened after the restoration of Charles II in 1660. The first recorded performance by a professional actress was Margaret Hughes as Desdemona in *The Moor Of Venice* on 3rd December 1660.

Drury Lane became the first theatre in Britain to be entirely lit by gas on 6th September 1817, although the Lyceum had introduced gas lighting for the stage just one month earlier.

The first use of a curtain coincided with the arrival of the proscenium arch, when theatres reopened in 1660. Initially the curtain was only raised at the beginning of the performance and lowered at the end. From the 1750s it was also lowered in the interval. The first use of a curtain being dropped to denote the end of a scene (and hide scenery changes) was pioneered by Henry Irving in a production of *The Corsican Brothers* at the Lyceum in 1881. He later introduced the blackout scene change.

The Royal Shakespeare Company staged the plays with the longest and shortest titles in the same season at the Aldwych in 1964. *The Persecution And Assassination Of Marat As Performed By The Inmates Of The Asylum Of Charenton Under The Direction Of The Marquis De Sade* by Peter Weiss is known for short as *The Marat/Sade*. Even so it is still not as short as Henry Livings *Eh?* (or *US* which they performed in 1966).

The World's shortest play is Samuel Beckett's *Breath* (1969) which lasts just 30 seconds.

The most prolific British playwright is Alan Ayckbourn whose Damsels in Distress trilogy - *Game Plan*, *Flat Spin* and *RolePlay* - his 48th, 49th and 50th plays, premiered in 2001. In 1975 he had five plays running simultaneously in London, *The Norman Conquests* (a trilogy), *Absurd Person Singular* and *Absent Friends*. In 2000 his two plays *House* and *Garden* were performed simultaneously with the same cast in the Lyttleton and Olivier auditoria at the National Theatre.

The actor most associated with a particular role was Richard Goolden as Mole in *Toad Of Toad Hall*, the stage version of A A Milne's *Wind In The Willows*, which was produced regularly each Christmas. He first played it at the Lyric in 1930 and finally at the Old Vic in 1979.

At the Richmond theatre in 1787 a Mr Cubit, the actor playing Hamlet, was taken ill in his dressing room immediately before a performance. There being no understudy, the manager (not wishing to refund the admissions) announced that the company would perform the play omitting the character of Hamlet. Sir Walter Scott, who was in the audience, noted that many of his fellow spectators considered the result to be a great improvement.

The Stage is the world's oldest weekly theatre trade paper having first appeared on 31st January 1880.

Fires

The Theatre Royal, Drury Lane is so called because its entrance was originally in Drury Lane. It has been rebuilt three times - twice because it burned down. During the rebuilding the orientation of the theatre was turned through 180 degrees so that the stage now backs on to Drury Lane and the entrance is in Catherine Street. As the third theatre burnt down on 24th February 1809, its then owner, the playwright Sheridan, observed proceedings from a nearby tavern. When asked how he could bear to watch his fortune and livelihood going up in smoke he replied "Tis a great pity if a man may not take a drink at his own fireside".

The Royal Opera House Covent Garden has also been twice destroyed by fire, and in one rebuilding its orientation was turned through 90 degrees. When gas lighting was first introduced at Covent Garden the gas was manufactured and stored in the building. After an explosion on 18th November 1828, the theatre reverted to illumination by oil lamp to allay public fears.

Henry Irving finally left the Lyceum in 1902 because a fire destroyed the warehouse in which he stored the sets and costumes he had amassed during his years as a producer, and he did not have sufficient funds to replace them.

Fires became such frequent occurrences in London theatres, that from 1855 the licensing authority ordered the annual inspection of theatres. This was to ensure "1 - Suitable methods of egress, 2 - Sufficient ventilation, 3 - Available and working extinguishers, 4 - General cleanliness".

John Gielgud directed and starred in *The Winter's Tale* at the Phoenix Theatre in 1951, during which Hazel Terry accidentally set herself alight and had to be doused by fellow actor (and later playwright) John Whiting. Gielgud remarked "I hear cousin Hazel caught fire. The Terry's have always been combustible."

WHY BREAK A LEG?

Superstitions

Most theatrical superstitions and traditions are shrouded in mystery and have no single explanation of their origins.

Bad Dress Rehearsal – Wishing an actor a bad dress rehearsal is based on the theory that a good dress rehearsal will lead to over confidence and result in a poor first night performance. When I worked with the director John Dexter, on the afternoon of the first night he insisted on running the whole play scene by scene in reverse order. He said it confused the cast sufficiently to make them really concentrate at the performance. Same idea.

Break A Leg – To directly wish someone Good Luck on the first night of a play is considered a jinx and so the phrase Break A Leg is used instead. Americans believe this is derives from John Wilkes Booth breaking his leg while trying to escape after assassinating Abraham Lincoln, but I can't see where good luck comes into that. Europeans think that it originated from a Yiddish greeting that was used by German airmen during World War I, being the equivalent of Happy Landings, which sounded like the German for 'break a leg'. From there it was translated into English and adopted by British airmen, and then by actors. Neither explanation seems very convincing.

Cats (Good Luck/Bad Luck) – Many theatres have cats (largely because all theatres have mice). One cat was always an investor in the shows that came into his theatre (the crew helped with the paperwork) and did quite nicely out of it. The Adelphi had two who were called Plug and Socket. It is good luck if a cat appears on stage during rehearsals - but bad luck if it appears during a performance. However this has not been borne out by my experience. The only time I have known it happen during a performance was in *Show Boat*, when either Plug or Socket (I can't remember which) walked across the jetty and then lay down and stretched out on the front deck. The show ran for four years.

Falling Down On The First Entrance – If an actor falls down on his first entrance it is considered to be lucky, based on the premise that nothing worse can happen during the rest of the performance.

Inside Out – If an actor puts on an item of costume or clothing inside out it must be worn that way for the rest of the performance or day because to change it brings bad luck.

Her Majestys Theatre, Wig Room

Knitting On Stage Or In The Wings – Everyone knows it brings bad luck – but no one knows why.

Leaving Soap In The Dressing Room – Apparently if an actor leaves a bar of soap in the dressing room at the end of a run he will never come back. This sounds like an excuse for frugality to me.

Not Saying The Last Line – There is a theory that you are not supposed to say the last line of a play until the first night, a belief dating back to Elizabethan times, in order not to tempt the Gods, as anything which is finished invites disaster. I have never come across anyone who abided by this. It is more likely to bring a technical disaster if the final sequence hasn't been rehearsed properly.

Peacock Feathers – Peacock feathers should never be used in a fan or costume trimming, or be represented in the set, because the eye of the peacock is thought to be an evil one. The set of *Chu Chin Chow*, the first record breaking musical in 1916, had peacocks painted on panelling in the original set design, but they were replaced by turkeys at the last minute. Make what you can will of that.

Putting Shoes On The Dressing Table – I don't know why it is supposed to be unlucky, or more to the point, how to counteract it – so best not do it.

Real Flowers On Stage – It is claimed to be unlucky to have real flowers on stage, supposedly in case the petals wilt and drop to the floor on which a performer might slip. I think it more likely to be a tale put about by producers as an excuse for making one fake bunch of flowers last an entire run.

The Scottish Play – It is regarded as unlucky to utter the word Macbeth, and so it is always referred to as 'the Scottish play', and the leading characters as 'Mr M' and 'Mrs M'. If mentioned in a dressing room the bad luck can be counteracted by leaving the room, turning round three times anti-clockwise (this represents turning back time) and knocking on the door three times to ask for readmittance. Variations include swearing and spitting. Quoting "angels and ministers of grace defend us" can also help. The play's ill-starred reputation may date from its first performance in 1606 when the boy actor playing Mrs M was taken ill an hour before it started and died before it was completed. There have been productions that have been dogged by bad luck, but these are a reinforcement of the legend rather than its cause. Some people believe that the witches' incantation at the beginning means that it is cursed.

Others that it is a victim of its popularity with the public in the 19th century. Whenever a play failed and a guaranteed crowd puller was needed as a substitute, The Scottish Play always fitted the bill. Thus if you mentioned the name it might be needed to do just that.

Spilling Wine – The origin is believed to be religious, but exactly why is unknown. The ill fortune is counteracted by putting your finger in the spilt wine and rubbing it behind your ear.

Thread On A Costume – Someone other than the wearer must take it off, and then the wearer should wind it round his forefinger. The number of revolutions indicates how long the run will be - or alternatively how long until his next contract.

Unlucky Tune – I Dreamt I Dwelt In Marble Halls, a song from the *Bohemian Girl*, was allegedly the piece being played on board the Titanic when it struck the iceberg and should not be whistled, sung or hummed in case it invites a similar catastrophe to the show.

Unpacking Make-Up – Some actors will not unpack their make-up box until after the notices are out, not wanting to presume that they will be in residence very long.

Wearing A Green Costume – One explanation for this superstition is that limelight had a greenish tinge and this combined with a green costume would render the actor invisible or make him look like a ghost.

Whistling In The Dressing Room – This is supposed to conjure up an ill wind resulting in a short run. It can be counteracted by leaving the room, turning round three times (anti-clockwise) and being invited back in.

Whistling On Stage – Before the days of sound or light communications, the stage manager used to whistle to the stage staff above in the flies to give the cue to drop in a piece of scenery (on the same principal as a sheep dog). Anyone whistling could therefore start the scenery moving at the wrong moment and injure someone - possibly himself. However a character in *The Mousetrap* has been whistling every night since 1952 and it hasn't done that show much harm.

I Told You So! – *The Clock Goes Round* at the Gielgud Theatre in 1913 challenged superstition by opening on Friday 13th, with thirteen characters, one wearing a green dress and carrying a fan of peacock feathers. Naturally the play closed after its thirteenth performance.

Traditions

The Baddeley Cake – In 1794 an actor called Robert Baddeley, who had played Moses in the first performance of Sheridan's *School for Scandal* at Drury Lane in 1777, left £100 to be invested to provide a cake and wine for the company playing there every Twelfth Night. With the exception of years during Word War II, the Baddeley Cake has been eaten on 6th January each year ever since, and the benefactor's memory toasted.

Billing – Believe it or not there are more arguments over billing, that is the size and placement of actors names on posters and flyers, than there are over money. This issue complicated by there being two prime positions, being billed above any one else, and being billed on the left (as this is the first thing people read). That is why you sometimes see ridiculous compromises where the name on the right is positioned higher than the name on the left.

Burnt Sugar Solution – This is the brown food dye which is diluted to make prop drinks such as whisky, brandy and sherry. Champagne makers Moet & Chandon supply prop champagne in authentic bottles with a lemonade substitute that is quite a pleasant drink.

Call Board – This is the notice board at the stage door where Calls (as actors working sessions are referred to) are posted. These can be rehearsal calls (which may be dance calls or vocal calls), photo calls, band calls - even a rehearsal call for the curtain calls. These notices still observe a traditional formality by referring to people as 'Miss X' and 'Mr Y'. The same formality pertains in announcements: "Miss Z your call please".

Call Boy – Before the days of tannoy systems, a call boy was employed to go round the dressing rooms to call actors to the stage for their entrances. This tradition is still maintained at the Haymarket Theatre, where the last remaining call boy in Britain is employed.

The First Rehearsal – This is when the cast and the creative team all meet for the first time. The set and costume designs are displayed, the script read and the songs sung. It is the ultimate sales pitch. The director sells the script, and the concept of how the show is to be realised to the cast, and the producer sells the whole package to himself, since he is already committed to spending a significant amount of other people's money. With new work it may be the first time the cast has seen a complete script. The danger signal is when they immediately call their agent at the end of the reading to try to get out of the engagement. I once saw that happen during the coffee break at the interval. There is always a nervous head count of those returning from lunch.

Green Room – The Green Room is a common room where actors can meet, although space is usually at a premium so few theatres actually have them. The first reference to one appears in Thomas Shadwell's play *A True Widow* in 1678. As to why they are so called, one explanation is that they were painted green because it is a relaxing colour – but I've never seen one that was green. More likely it is because actors refer to the stage as 'the green' – hence their parting remark at the end of rehearsals "See you on the green". Thus the room next to 'the green' was the Green Room. Now why do they call the stage 'the green'? If you find out the answer let me know.

Has The Ghost Walked? – This is a euphemism for "has the manager distributed the pay packets?" It is believed to derive from the fact that actor managers often played the role of the Ghost in *Hamlet* because it allowed them plenty of free time off stage to deal with the box office returns, make up the wage packets, and pay the cast.

In The Limelight – Limelight was a pre-electricity method of lighting, invented by Captain Thomas Drummond in 1816. It was created by playing a high temperature flame onto a piece of lime causing it to glow very brightly. Contained in some sort of housing, the light could be directed at the stage and used to follow the leading actor, making him/her stand out from the others on stage. Although no longer using lime, the basic principle was employed in early film projectors, and was still used in follow spots until fairly recently.

Last Night Practical Jokes – Frustrations built up during a run are often released by playing tricks on fellow artists at the final performance. These take a variety of forms, including tampering with food and drink, gluing shut things which have to be opened, putting stage weights in suitcases, and substituting props – such as replacing cigars in a box with hot dog sausages.

Masks of Comedy and Tragedy – The masks showing smiling or grimacing faces derive from the theatre of ancient Greece, in which all the actors wore masks denoting the sex, age, social standing and mood of the character they were playing. In recent years opera has been accused of wearing a third mask - Snobbery.

Pass Door – This is the only connection between the Front Of House – the public part of the theatre – and Backstage – the performers' domain. Depending on the construction of the building, sometimes this is a very obvious door marked Private just outside the entrance to the stalls or stalls boxes, sometimes it is a concealed door in the wall of stalls itself. Usually you will see the company manager go through it to the stage to start the show once the audience is seated and the auditorium doors have been closed.

Patent Theatres – On 2nd September 1642, during the Civil War, all theatres were closed by parliamentary decree. Following the restoration of Charles II in 1660, Thomas Killigrew and William Davenant were granted a monopoly of theatrical affairs. After some difficulties, in 1662 the King issued them with Patents granting permission to create companies to perform plays. Killigrew formed The King's Servants and built Drury Lane for them to perform in. Davenant established The Duke Of York's Servants in a converted tennis court in Lincoln's Inn Fields. His Patent was transferred to Covent Garden in 1732. A third seasonal Patent, which allowed plays to be performed in the summer when the other theatres were closed, was granted to Samuel Foote at the Haymarket in 1766. The Theatres Act of 1843 broke the monopoly of Patent theatres allowing any theatre to perform plays.

Pickfords – In one of the last remaining examples of restrictive industrial practices in Britain, actors who move furniture during scene changes are entitled to receive an extra per performance payment. This is known as Pickfords after the famous removals company.

Surprise Pink – A colour filter that was traditionally known to help actresses of a certain age to regain their youthful looks. The surprise is that although its real name (Pale Lavender) accurately describes its colour, when artificial light shines through it the result is an enhancing pink.

Thespians – Thespis was a writer, actor and producer in ancient Greece, and the winner of the first ever play competition in 534BC. He is credited with introducing the first solo actor to the theatre, which until then had been conducted entirely by a chorus. Thus the solo actors in his company became known as Thespians.

Trap – An opening in the stage floor. A Grave Trap is a rectangle large enough to take a coffin (as used in *Hamlet*). A Star Trap is circular and made up of triangular sprung leaves opening upwards so that an actor can be propelled through from underneath the stage to magically appear usually accompanied by a puff of smoke). A Vampire Trap is circular and made up of two sprung leaves opening downwards so that an actor can sink through the stage to magically disappear (usually accompanied by a puff of smoke).

Twofer – As in 'Two for the price of one'. Although this is generally acknowledged to be a New York invention, a Privilege Ticket, granting two seats for the price of one, was introduced at the Aldwych Theatre in the late 1930s.

Walter Plinge – The pseudonym used for disguise purposes in billing and programmes. For instance, if the producer doesn't want the audience to know that one actor plays two parts or wants to give the impression that there are more actors in the play than there really are.

Technical Terms/Slang

Beginners – an actor's call to the stage five minutes before the show/act starts.

Cans – headset and microphone unit used by stage managers to communicate with the technicians during a performance.

Civilians - people outside the theatrical profession.

Chanters – chorus singers.

Corpse – be unable to speak because of laughing.

Dark – a theatre which does not have a show on (i.e. its exterior lights are off).

The Dots - sheet music.

Dry – forget the script.

Frocks – costumes.

Hoofers – chorus dancers.

The Half – the time by which actors must be at the theatre, 35 minutes before the show starts (half an hour before Beginners).

Noise Boys – sound operators.

Prompt Corner – where the stage manager controls the show, traditionally stage left.

Sitzprobe - imported German term for the first artists rehearsal with an orchestra.

Tabs – main curtain, originally 'tableaux curtains' which drew outwards and upwards as those at the London Palladium still do.

Walk Downs – the curtain calls when people take their bows.

Walking Understudies - understudies who are not actually in the show.

Waving – what the person conducting the orchestra does.

Winging – improvising when you have forgotten the script.

First Nights: "Darling You Were Wonderful"

A couple at the rear of the stalls at the end of a disastrous first night.

She: Well I suppose we'd better go round.

He: Do we have to?

She: Of course we do.

He: Why?

She: Because you're the director and I'm the choreographer.

W S Gilbert is generally credited with the immortal line "My dear fellow! Good isn't the word!" Another school claims it for Oscar Wilde, talking to Herbert Beerbohm Tree on his performance as Hamlet in 1892. But then on a different occasion when Wilde exclaimed "I wish I'd said that" he received the repost "You will Oscar, you will".

Henry Irving's comment to American actor Richard Mansfield when he complained about the strain of playing both Dr Jekyll and Mr Hyde was "if it's unendurable, why do it?"

It was W S Gilbert who after witnessing Arthur Bourchier's Hamlet said "at last we can settle whether Bacon or Shakespeare wrote the plays. Have both the coffins opened and whoever has turned in his grave is the author."

Ned Sherrin entered a distinguished actress's dressing room with "You were wonderful – but you can take off that dreadful false nose now" only to receive the response "I already have".

The best line I have heard personally is "You did it again!" which of course could mean absolutely anything.

When people are at a loss for words, they usually take refuge in being overly enthusiastic about the scenery and costumes, one person is believed to have ventured "The brass-work in the stalls was beautifully polished". At all costs try to avoid "Oh, but you looked so beautiful on stage".

It is considered unlucky for a visitor to enter a dressing room left foot first. Anyone who does so must exit backwards and re-enter right foot first.

Prince Edward Theatre, Dressing Room

Ghosts

Adelphi – The actor William Terris was murdered outside the Royal Entrance in Maiden Lane (where the stage door is now) by rival actor Richard Archer in 1897. He is said to haunt Bullen Court, the alley that runs alongside the theatre linking the Strand and Maiden Lane (where the stage door was then) wearing a frock coat and top hat.

Duke Of York's – An iron fire door that was removed many decades ago is heard to slam every night at ten o'clock. Some years ago an old fashioned key with a tag marked Iron Door dropped at the feet of the manager.
A female figure dressed in black has been seen wandering through the circle bar. It is said to be the ghost of Violet Melnotte the original owner, known to everyone as 'Madame'.

Drury Lane – The Man In Grey, a gentleman in 18th century riding cloak, boots, sword and tricorn hat, walks through one wall at the end of row D, across the upper circle, and disappears into the wall on the other side. The appearance usually occurs during matinees and is considered a sign of good fortune. He is thought to be connected with a skeleton found with a dagger in its ribs bricked up in the wall through which he disappears.
Another ghost, believed to be that of the clown Grimaldi, who gave his farewell appearance at the theatre in 1828, administers a kick up the backside to actors giving bad performances.
The reflection of comedian and comic actor Dan Leno has been seen in the mirror of his favourite dressing room.
Actor manager Charles Macklin fatally stabbed a fellow actor called Hallam in the eye with a stick in an argument over a wig in the Green Room in 1735. Macklin was convicted of manslaughter but avoided imprisonment by paying a fine to Hallam's family. He stalks the area that used to be the pit.

Garrick – Actors descending a staircase from the dressing rooms to the stage (known as the Phantom Staircase) have reported feeling a slap on the back by way of encouragement from the ghost of actor manager Arthur Bourchier.
The Garrick also has a phantom prompter who whispers lines from the old prompt corner.

Haymarket – John Buckstone, the 19th century actor manager, is said to have loved the theatre so much that he can't bear to leave it. He has been seen many times in the star dressing room, entering through a bricked up former doorway, and also on stage during performances. Because of his great success as a manager this is considered to be a good omen.

Her Majesty's – The actor manager Herbert Beerbohm Tree, who built the current theatre, has been observed making his way from the Dome rooms, where he kept an apartment, to his favourite box.

St George's Hall – John Neville Maskelyne, of the famous conjuring and magic family, has been spotted on stage performing the plate spinning act which made his name.

Fly Floor, London Palladium

THEATRE ARCHITECTS

Bertie Crewe (d 1937)

Lyceum (interior), Phoenix (with Sir Giles Gilbert Scott and Cecil Masey), Piccadilly (with Edward A Stone), Royal Court (with Walter Emden), Shaftesbury

Apprenticed to Clement Dowling and Frank Matcham in London, Bertie Crewe also spent some time with Atelier Laloux in Paris working on buildings such as the Gare D'Orsay. He specialised entirely in theatres, and later cinemas. After a period of relatively restrained work with Phipps, he developed a flamboyant style with Baroque touches and a delight in elaborate, even extravagant decoration that was completely three dimensional. Crewe was particularly skilled in creating impressive façades that matched the theatricality of their interiors. With the Stoll theatre, probably his greatest work, he created a magnificent opera house in the continental fashion.

London Palladium

Walter Emden (1847-1913)
Duke of York's, Garrick (with C J Phipps), Royal Court (with Bertie Crewe)
The son of a theatre proprietor Walter Emden began as a scenic designer, before studying civil engineering and finally architecture at Kelly and Lawes. Probably betraying his lack of formal training, Emden's early work displayed a vast range of styles. Terry's theatre looked like a public house, while the Tivoli had the appearance of a palace of varieties. His later work was more restrained, with the Duke of York's looking like a grand private house, and the Garrick boasting a classically inspired colonnade. Emden also designed many restaurants, hotels and other places of entertainment.

Frank Matcham (1854-1920)
Coliseum, London Palladium, Victoria Palace, Hackney Empire, Richmond Theatre
Frank Matcham was the most prolific and innovative theatre architect the world has known. He was born in Newton Abbot, the son of a brewery manager, and was apprenticed to George S Bridgeman, a local architect, where he discovered his love for theatre architecture. Matcham went to work in the practice of Jethro T Robinson, who was Consulting Theatre Architect to the Lord Chamberlain, and in 1877 married Robinson's daughter Maria. Robinson's unexpected death the following year opened the way for Matcham to take over one of the most prestigious architectural practices in London at the age of 24. His work rate was prodigious, and by 1880 he had become the most sought after theatre architect in the country specialising in the larger and more extravagant music halls, lyric theatres and opera houses. Only nine of his thirty theatres survive, but they illustrate his talent for handsome decoration and excellent sightlines. Matcham's greatest technical innovation was in pioneering the use of the cantilevered auditorium, thus eliminating the need for pillars to support the circles.

C J Phipps (1897-1935)
Garrick (with Walter Emden), Her Majesty's, Lyric, Vaudeville (exterior)
Born in Bath, Charles John Phipps was articled to local architects Wilcox and Fuller, before starting his own practice, and then moving to London in 1863. He was a prolific designer of theatres, hotels, apartment blocks and public buildings. Phipps specialised in play houses rather than lyric theatres or music halls, which are characterised by restraint and low relief decoration in contrast to the flamboyance of Matcham or Crewe. His early work lent towards the Gothic and ecclesiastical, but he later adopted a more classical style. His exteriors exude a solid civic dignity, Her Majesty's, showing his partiality for French theatrical design, could almost be an Hotel de Ville.

W G R Sprague (1865-1933)

Albery, Aldwych, Gielgud, New Ambassadors, Queen's, St Martin's, Strand, Wyndhams

Sprague was born in Australia to an English actress Dolores Drummond, who returned to England in 1874. At 16 he was apprenticed to Matcham for four years, and then to Emden for a further three before setting up on his own. Continued study ensured that he was probably the best trained architect of the period with great breadth of technical and stylistic knowledge. Unlike many others, he ensured that his exteriors were at one with his interiors. Sprague specialised in intimate and elegant play houses, influenced by 19th century French style, but in his own distinctive manner. His particular forte was twin theatres with subtle variations.

Edward A Stone

Piccadilly (with Bertie Crewe), Prince Edward, Whitehall

Edward Stone was one of the most successful designers of cinemas and cine-theatres, some of which had impressive provision for stage shows. He was of a later generation than the other major architects, producing Art Deco influenced buildings. It was frequently his practice to entrust the interiors of his theatres to specialists. Stone's work also included the Astorias at Brixton (now Academy) and Finsbury Park (now Rainbow) whose 'atmospheric' design schemes feature lavishly detailed Mediterranean and Arabian townscapes surrounding the prosceniums and decorating the side walls of the auditoria, and night sky ceilings with twinkling stars.

Thomas Verity (1837-1891)

Comedy, Criterion

Thomas Verity was articled to an architect employed by the War Office, working on the South Kensington Museum, and was principal assistant on the design of the Royal Albert Hall 1867-70. He won a competition to design the Criterion restaurant and concert hall that later became a theatre. From 1870 to his death he was Consulting Theatre Architect to the Lord Chamberlain. A great Francophile, his theatres show the influence of French Second Empire and later the Beaux-Arts tradition. The interior scheme of decorated ceramic tiles and mirrors of the Criterion is unique. Verity also designed many non theatrical buildings.

ACT I - THE THEATRES

1.1 Theatreland Map

1.2 Theatre Information
History, location, facilities, and seating plan for each of
the West End theatres

1.3 Other Venues
Theatres Beyond The West End, Fringe Theatres,
Specialist Theatres and Concert Halls

THEATRE INFORMATION

Key

🎭	Address
☎	Box Office Number
🖰	Website
⊖	Tube
🚌	Bus
🚆	Train
Ⓟ	Car Parking
✹	Air Conditioned
◁	Infra-red/Loop Sound Amplification System
♿	Wheelchair Access
▲	Steps Up to Level
▼	Steps Down to Level
🪑	Seating Capacity
☆	Special Feature

Duchess

THEATRELAND MAP

1 Royal Opera House
2 Fortune
3 Theatre Royal Drury Lane
4 Duchess

5 Strand
6 Aldwych
7 Lyceum
8 Savoy
9 Vaudeville
10 Adelphi
11 Playhouse
12 Whitehall
13 Coliseum
14 Duke of York's
15 Albery
16 Arts
17 Wyndham's
18 Garrick
19 tkts-Official Half Price Ticket
    Booth
20 Prince of Wales
21 Comedy
22 Theatre Royal Haymarket
23 Her Majesty's
24 Criterion
25 Piccadilly
26 Lyric
27 Apollo
28 Gielgud
29 Queen's
30 Palace
31 Prince Edward

32 Phoenix
33 Dominion
34 Shaftesbury
35 New Ambassadors
36 St Martins
37 Cambridge
38 Donmar Warehouse
39 Phoenix

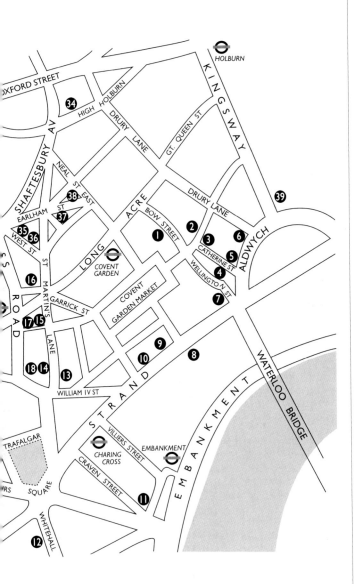

Adelphi

🖂 *The Strand, WC2R 0NS*

☎ *020 7344 0055*

⊖ *Charing Cross / Covent Garden / Leicester Square*

🚌 *6, 9, 11, 13, 15, 23, 77A, 91, 176*

🚉 *Charing Cross* Ⓟ *Bedfordbury / Trafalgar Square*

✈ *Air Condition* ◁ *Infra-red*

♿ *Stalls / Dress Circle Box*

☆ *Stalls bars contain displays of memorabilia relating to Vivian Ellis and Jessie Matthews*

There have been theatres on this site since 1806 when John Scott built the Sans Parallel for his daughter to perform in, opening with *Miss Scott's Entertainments*. It was renamed the Adelphi after its 1819 refurbishment, when it became one of the first London theatres to be lit by a gas chandelier. In 1834 the first mechanical sinking stage in Britain was installed. Popular theatre, musicals or light entertainment, have been its staple. The original license was for the presentation of 'burlettas' - dramas that included at least five pieces of vocal music in each act. As a result even Othello had piano accompaniment when it was presented here. The present building, designed by Ernest Schaufelberg in 1930, is notable for its Art Deco style and the complete absence of curves in its construction. Straight lines and angles dominate the theatre's decorative scheme both inside and out. The exterior is remarkable for its large irregular octagon window at first floor level, restored in 1993, and the foyer for its black marble walls and chrome fittings. Dramatic versions of Dickens novels were presented here almost as soon as they appeared in print, including *Nicholas Nickleby*, *Oliver Twist* and *A Christmas Carol* (1837-45). In 1897 the actor William Terris was murdered by a jealous rival as he was entering the theatre by the Royal Entrance in Maiden Lane. The early years of the twentieth century saw a succession of operettas and musicals including *The Quaker Girl* (1908), Gladys Cooper in *Peter Pan* (1923), Evelyn Laye in *Betty In Mayfair* (1925), and Vivian Ellis's *Mr Cinders* (1929) with Binnie Hale and Bobby Howes. Under the management of Charles B Chocrane it became a home for revue with Jessie Matthews in *Evergreen* (1930), Noel Coward's *Words And Music* (1932). Cole Porter's *Nymph Errant* (1933), A P Herbert's *Home And Beauty* (1937), Ivor Novello's *The Dancing Years* (1942), and *Bless The Bride* (1947) followed. During the 1950s there were a succession of variety shows featuring radio and television stars. Musicals returned with Lionel Bart's *Blitz!* (1962) which became famous as the show where "people came out humming the scenery" and *Maggie May* (1964), Anna Neagle in *Charlie Girl* (1965), *Show Boat* (1971), Stephen Sondheim's *A Little Night Music* (1975), *Me And My Girl* (1985) and most recently Andrew Lloyd Webber's *Sunset Boulevard* (1993).

Adelphi

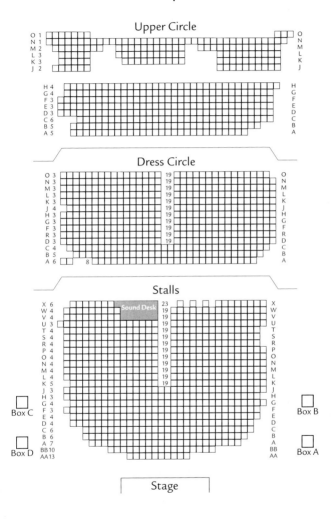

Upper Circle

Dress Circle

Stalls

Sound Desk

Box C
Box D

Box B
Box A

Stage

79▲ Upper Circle, 41▲ Dress Circle, 0▲ Stalls, 1▲ Foyer, ♿1478

25

Albery

⌨ *St Martin's Lane, WC2N 4AH*
☎ *020 7369 1730*
🖎 *www.theambassadors.com*
⊖ *Leicester Square*
🚌 *24, 29, 176*
🚆 *Charing Cross* ⓟ *Upper St Martin's Lane/Bedfordbury*
✱ *Air Condition* ◀ *Infra-red*
♿ *Dress Circle Box*
☆ *Bridge at the rear links to Wyndhams so that if one theatre has a large cast and there is spare room in the other actors can dress there*

Actor manager Charles Wyndham built this theatre in 1903, as a larger and grander companion to the existing theatre in Charing Cross Road that still bears his name. Both theatres were designed by W G R Sprague and sit back to back with similar French classical façades. The Albery's auditorium has a Louis XVI inspired cream and gold decorative scheme, with cameos on the side walls at circle levels and two gold angels representing Peace and Music attended by cupids illustrating Winter and Summer above the proscenium. It was originally known as the New theatre – Wyndham couldn't decide what to call it, so it was referred to as the new theatre during construction, and the name stuck. The New became the Albery in 1973 when Wyndham's successors, the Albery family named it in honour of their grandfather, the impresario Sir Bronson Albery. The Albery has generally been the home for star studded revivals of classic plays and West End seasons by other producing companies. Wyndham and his wife Mary Moore appeared in the opening production *Rosemary*. Among the works to have premiered here were Noel Coward's first play *I'll Leave It To You* (1920) with Coward in the lead, George Bernard Shaw's *St Joan* (1924) with Sybil Thorndike, T S Eliot's *The Cocktail Party* (1950), and Lionel Bart's *Oliver* (1960) – its longest running success at 2618 performances. John Gielgud established himself as a star in *Hamlet* (1934) with the second longest run of the play ever, and *Romeo And Juliet* (1935) in which he and Laurence Olivier alternated the roles of Romeo and Mercutio. From 1941 to 1950 the Sadler's Wells and Old Vic companies moved in to present plays, opera and ballet, having lost their homes due to bomb damage. Productions included Ralph Richardson as *Peer Gynt* (1944), Olivier and Richardson in *Uncle Vanya* (1946) and Edith Evans in *The Cherry Orchard* (1948). The new National Theatre company presented a season here in 1971 with Laurence Olivier in *Long Day's Journey Into Night*, *Danton's Death* and *Rules Of The Game*. More recently the Almeida Theatre made The Albery their West End home with *Phèdre*, *Britannicus*, *Vassa* and *Plenty* (1998-99).

Albery

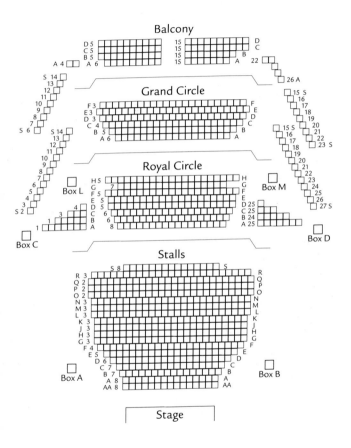

Balcony

Grand Circle

Royal Circle

Box L   Box M

Box C   Box D

Stalls

Box A   Box B

Stage

55▲ Balcony, 30▲ Upper Circle, 3▲ Dress Circle, 30▼ Stalls, 3▲ Foyer, 🔍 877

27

Aldwych

⌨ *The Aldwych, WC2B 4DF*

☎ *0870 4000 805*

⊖ *Covent Garden / Holborn / Temple*

🚌 *1, 4, 6, 9, 11, 13, 15, 23, 26, 59, 68, 76, 77A, 91, 168, 171, 172,*

🚆 *Charing Cross*

Ⓟ *Drury Lane / Bedfordbury Street*

✈ *Air Condition*

♿ *Dress Circle*

☆ *Foyer shares a two storey high ceiling and chandelier with the Dress Circle bar similar to the Gielgud*

The Aldwych was designed by W G R Sprague as a twin to the Strand theatre. Both were built in 1905 when the new street The Aldwych was being laid out and 'bookend' the block accompanied by the Waldorf hotel. The Aldwych has a classical façade in Portland stone with pediments and columns while its interior combines Georgian and French Baroque. The decorative scheme of grey-blue with gilt ornamentation suffered during the "paint it black" era of the Royal Shakespeare Company but has since been restored. Although musical comedies with Seymour Hicks and Ellaline Terriss were a feature of the Aldwych's early years, it was a series of farces which really put the theatre on the map. The Aldwych Farces, as they became known, were written by Ben Travers and included legendary plays such as *A Cookoo In The Nest* (1925), *Rookery Nook* (1926), *Dirty Work* (1932) and *A Bit Of A Test* (1933). Tom Walls and Ralph Lynn appeared in all of them supported by a company that included Mary Brough, Winifred Shorter and Robertson Hare. The Aldwych enjoyed a second, very different golden age between 1960 and 1982 when it became the London home of the Royal Shakespeare Company. Many Shakespeare productions transferred here from Stratford during the directorships of Peter Hall and Trevor Nunn, including the eight play history cycle, *The Wars Of The Roses* (1965), and Peter Brook's *A Midsummer Night's Dream* (1971). These alternated with a modern drama repertory that included *The Marat / Sade*, Jules Feifer's *Little Murders*, and *US*. Another landmark production was *Nicholas Nickleby* (1979). Every summer between 1964–1973 the Aldwych played host to some of the world's greatest theatres companies, courtesy of Peter Daubney's World Theatre Seasons. The Aldwych saw the British premiers of Chekhov's *The Cherry Orchard* (1911), Tennessee Williams's *A Streetcar Named Desire* (1949) with Vivien Leigh, Anouilh's *Beckett* (1961) and Harold Pinter's *The Homecoming* (1965). In recent years a number of productions have transferred here from the National Theatre, among them Jim Cartwright's *The Rise And Fall Of Little Voice* (1992) with Jane Horrocks, J B Priestley's *An Inspector Calls* (1993) and David Hare's *Amy's View* (1998) with Judi Dench.

Aldwych

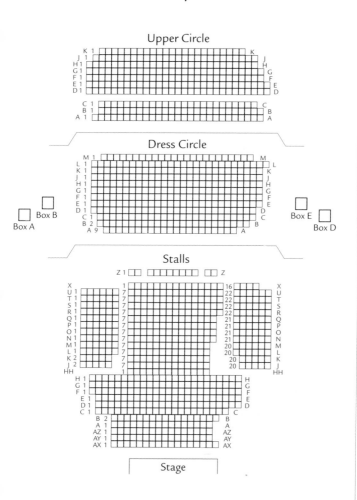

Upper Circle

Dress Circle

Box A · Box B · Box E · Box D

Stalls

Stage

24▲ Upper Circle, 15▲ Dress Circle, 26▼ Stalls, 6▲ Foyer, ♿ 1200

Apollo

⌨ *Shaftesbury Avenue, W1V 7DH*

☎ *020 7494 5070*

✍ *www.rutheatres.com*

⊖ *Piccadilly Circus*

🚌 *14, 19, 38*

🚃 *Charing Cross*

Ⓟ *Brewer Street / Denman Street*

✈ *Air Condition*   ◁ *Infra-red*

☆ *To the right of the entrance there is the coat of arms, a silver chain and buckle with a flying lizard supported by two lions rampant*

The only theatre designed by Lewen Sharp, the Apollo was envisaged as a home for musical entertainments, with an orchestra pit inspired by the opera house at Bayreuth, and much care given to the acoustics. In fact, ever since it opened in 1901, it has mostly housed light comedies, with musicals going to the slightly larger Lyric next door. Architecturally it is strikingly different from the other Shaftesbury Avenue theatres, with a façade in French renaissance style, and winged figures adorning the domed towers which make up its top story. The coat of arms at the entrance is the badge of a group of gypsies with whom Henry Lowenfeld, the original owner, was connected. This device was supposed to bring good luck and formed a major part of the original design scheme for the building, which at one stage was to have been called the Mascot. The auditorium, which is notable for its lack of pillars, is decorated in an opulent Louis XIV style, with statuary supporting the boxes. The first big success here was H G Pelisser's *The Follies* (1908-1912) which laid the foundations for intimate revue. Later revues were Jack Hulbert and Cicely Courteneidge in *By The Way* (1925), *For Amusement Only* (1956), and *Pieces Of Eight* (1959) with Kenneth Williams and Fenella Fielding. Marion Lorne starred in a series of plays written and produced for her by her husband Walter Hackett, including *Hyde Park Corner* (1934), and *London After Dark* (1937). Among the premieres it has seen are Harold Brighouse's *Hobson's Choice* (1916), Terence Rattigan's *Flare Path* (1942), *The Happiest Days Of Your Life* (1948) with Margaret Rutherford, Alan Bennett's *Forty Years On* (1968), Keith Waterhouse's *Jeffrey Bernard Is Unwell* (1989) with Peter O'Toole. Other notable productions include *Abie's Irish Rose* (1927), Sean O'Casey's *The Silver Tassie* (1929), Robert Sherwood's *Idiot's Delight* (1938) with Raymond Massey, and *Seagulls Over Sorrento* (1950). The Apollo's longest run was provided by Marc Camoletti's *Boeing-Boeing* (1962), which transferred after 3 years; more recently it has been home to another Camoletti farce, *Don't Dress For Dinner* (1991).

Apollo

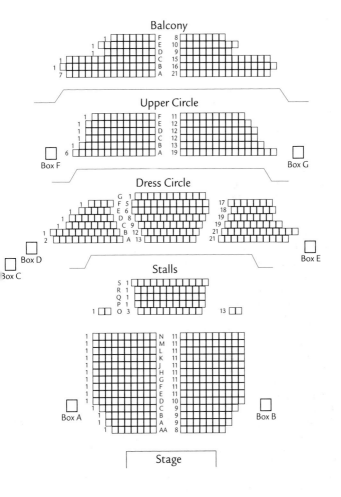

60▲ Balcony, 40▲ Upper Circle, 12▲ Dress Circle,
22▼ Stalls, 1▲ Foyer, ♿ 775

Apollo Victoria

⌨ *Wilton Road, SW1V 1LG*

☎ *0870 4000 650*

✉ *www.victoria-apollo.co.uk*

⊖ *Victoria*

🚌 *2, 8, 11, 16, 24, 36, 38, 52, 73, 82, 185, 239, 507, C1, C10*

🚃 *Victoria*

Ⓟ *Rochester Row/Vauxhall Bridge Road*

♿ *Dress Circle*

☆ *Fine Art Deco architectural details.*

The Apollo Victoria was originally built as a super cinema and opened in 1930, the golden age of architectural extravagance in picture palaces, as the New Victoria Cinema. One of the most architecturally important cinemas in Britain, it was the first to be built in the Germanic expressionist style. Its scale is grand, originally accommodating 2,500 people, with the stalls seating extending out under the pavements. The foyer spans the entire block with two entrances, one in Wilton Road and the other in Vauxhall Bridge Road. It was designed by E Wamsley Lewis with a modern marble and concrete exterior, which is ribbed like a gigantic radio set, and includes reliefs of cinemagoers by Newberry A Trent on either side of the Wilton Road entrance. The interior has an underwater theme, with fish, shells and sea flora motifs while the circle was designed like an ocean liner with portholes in the doors. Most of the sculpture and decorative work is by Trent and much of it remains today, including a bronze reclining mermaid in Cleopatra style above the entrance to the Gents, and a nude in the foyer juggling with reels of film. The venue was conceived as a cine-variety house and opened with a programme that comprised *Hoop-La*, a stage show, Reginald Foort at the organ, and the film *Old England*. Stage shows were soon dropped, but appearances by big bands and live acts continued throughout the 1930s. George V attended a Royal Charity matinée of *The Good Companions* here in 1933. Theatrical use began after its facilities were upgraded in 1958, with ad hoc concerts and later appearances by London Festival Ballet, as large cinemas went out of fashion. In 1972 it was the first cinema to achieve Listed Building status. It closed in 1976 and was relaunched as a full-time theatre bearing the name Apollo Victoria in 1981, with moderately successful revivals of *The Sound Of Music* (1981) *Camelot* (1982) and *Fiddler On The Roof* (1983). The auditorium was subsequently reconfigured, losing 1000 seats in the process, to accommodate the skating rink for *Starlight Express* (1984). This also resulted in some of the decorative features being removed, repainted or obscured. Following the closure of *Starlight Express* in January 2002, the auditorium has been sympathetically restored to its pre 1984 grandeur with many of the architectural features being uncovered and repaired.

Apollo Victoria

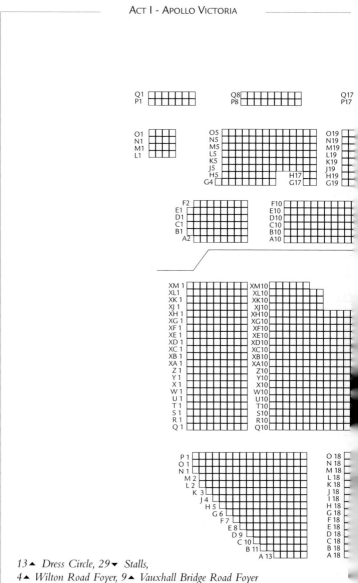

13▲ Dress Circle, 29▼ Stalls,
4▲ Wilton Road Foyer, 9▲ Vauxhall Bridge Road Foyer
🦋 *1524+40 standing*

Apollo Victoria

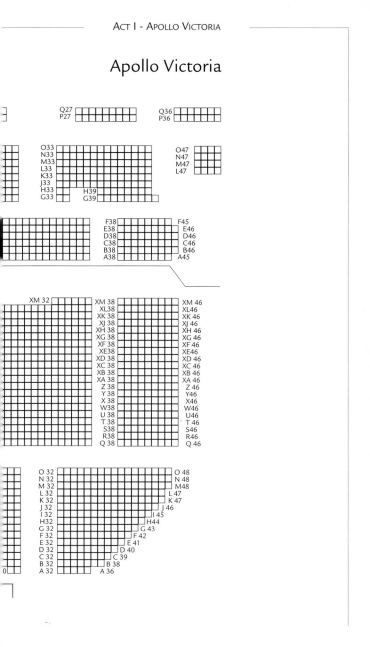

Arts

⌨ *Great Newport Street, WC1E 7HF*
☎ *020 7836 3334*
🖥 *www.artstheatre.com*
⊖ *Leicester Square*
🚌 *24, 29, 176*
🚃 *Charing Cross*
Ⓟ *Lisle Street/Upper St Martin's Lane*
♿ *Dress Circle*
☆ *Foyer coffee bar is open all day and has a small art exhibition*

The Arts was purpose-built in 1927 to a design by P Morley Horder as a
private club which included a small theatre. The original auditorium
was destroyed by fire in 1951, and is now rectangular with a small circle,
side slips, and virtually no decoration. It was established to provide a
space where unusual plays, often of limited general interest, could be
performed uncensored, as they would not need to be licensed by the
Lord Chamberlain. An early example was John Van Druten's *Young
Woodley* (1928), and other plays that went on to transfer to ordinary West
End theatres were Van Druten's *Diversion*, *The Lady With The Lamp* and
People Like Us. In 1942 actor Alec Clunes took over the management
and ran what amounted to a pocket National Theatre, with new plays,
revivals and seasons of English comedy. Premieres included Eugene
O'Neil's *The Ice Man Cometh* and Christopher Fry's *The Lady's Not For
Burning* (1948). Again the most successful transferred to West End
houses to earn revenue to keep the company running. A new regime
committed to new writing gave the world premiere of Samuel Beckett's
ground breaking *Waiting For Godot* (1955), and Jean Anouilh's *The Waltz
Of The Toreadors* (1956) both directed by Peter Hall. Harold Pinter's *The
Caretaker* (1960) also received its first production here. In *Lady
Chatterley's Lover* (1961) Jeanne Moody appeared naked, resulting in
questions being asked in the House of Commons – and the run extending by several months. When Peter Hall took over the Royal
Shakespeare Company this was its first London home, opening with
Everything In The Garden (1962) but the venture was not successful.
From 1966 until 1998 the Unicorn Theatre for Children was based here,
performing new work for young theatregoers during the day, with occasional runs of shows for adults presented by outside managements in the
evenings. A new company took over in 2000 and upgraded the facilities
so that it is no longer a club. Although its declared aim was to present
short runs of new works and revivals, it has so far only presented
commercial runs for touring productions of *Another Country* (2000) and
Entertaining *Mr Sloane* (2001) and the Pet Shop Boys musical, *Closer To
Heaven* (2001).

Arts

Dress Circle

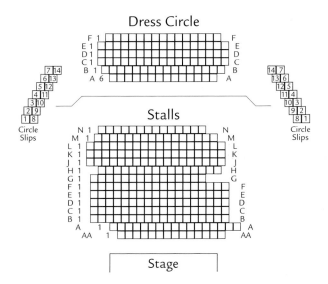

Stalls

Stage

5▲ Dress Circle, 19▼ Stalls, 0▲ Foyer, 🏛362

Barbican

⌨ *Silk Street, EC2Y 8BQ*
☎ *020 7638 8891*
🖰 *www.barbican.org.uk (RSC www.rsc.org.uk)*
⊖ *Moorgate/Barbican*
🚌 *4, 21, 43, 56, 76, 100, 133, 141, 271*
🚆 *Moorgate/Farringdon*
Ⓟ *Beneath the theatre*
✈ *Air Condition* ◁ᴵ *Infra-red*
☆ *Waterside restaurant, bookshop, pre-show entertainment, foyer open all day, conservatory and sculpture court on the roof*

Theatre

♿ *Stalls & Upper Circle Lift available*
20▲ Balcony
0▲ Upper Circle Lift available
16▼ Dress Circle
34▼ Stalls Lift available
34▼ Foyer Lift available
🦻*1162*

Pit

♿ *Stalls Lift available*
90▼ Stalls Lift available
90▼ Foyer Lift available
🦻 *185*

In 1959 the Corporation of the City of London agreed a scheme for a residential development with a theatre and concert hall for the Guildhall School of Music and Drama in an area that had been destroyed by bombing in World War II. In 1962 it was decided that the theatre and concert hall should be reserved for professional companies, and in 1964 the Royal Shakespeare Company and the London Symphony Orchestra became the designated companies, involved in the design. The residential development went ahead, but it took eighteen years and numerous changes of personnel, minds, and plans, alarming budgetary rises, near cancellations and conceptual revisions before it opened in 1982. By this time the planning vogue of the 1960s with its wholesale redevelopment of areas, eliminating street patterns and separating pedestrians from traffic with walkways had been discredited, but here was a scheme which did just that. It became a standing joke that no-one could find their way into the building, and when they did, they couldn't find the level of the theatre or concert hall they wanted. Various facelifts, signage schemes,

renumbering of levels and internal bridges have been tried by successive managerial regimes, but the struggle continues. In addition to the theatre and concert hall the centre finally included the Pit studio theatre, 3 cinemas, exhibition and conference facilities, an art gallery, a library and a conservatory spread over eight levels. The design by Chamberlin, Powell and Bon, provided an extensive foyer with the feeling of a hotel lounge. The theatre, a plain design finished in dark Peruvian walnut, is unusual in that seating is mostly in the stalls, with three circles of just two rows each having short side extensions thrust forward towards the stage. There are no aisles and each row is entered separately through doors that simultaneously woosh closed as the houselights dim. The Royal Shakespeare Company moved productions back and forth continuously between here and Stratford until 1997 when it decided to play here for only six months of the year. The Barbican then instituted the Barbican International Theatre Event, which brings theatre and dance companies from all over the world to play here from May to October each year. These have included Abbey Theatre Dublin, Comedie-Francaise, Ninagawa Company and Steppenwolf Theatre Chicago. The Royal Shakespeare Company will leave for good in 2002 and it remains to be seen how the Barbican will survive.

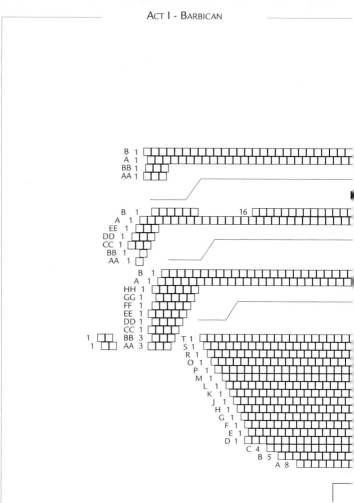

 ♿ *Stalls & Upper Circle Lift available*

20▲ *Balcony*

0▲ *Upper Circle Lift available*

16▼ *Dress Circle*

34▼ *Stalls Lift available*

34▼ *Foyer Lift available*

♿ 1162

Barbican Theatre

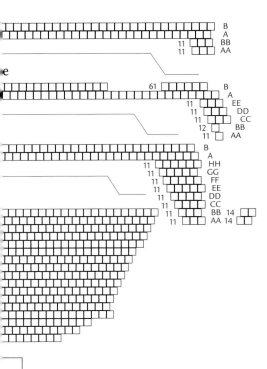

Cambridge

⌨ *Earlham Street, WC2 9HU*

☎ *020 7494 5080*

✍ *www.rutheatres.com*

⊖ *Leicester Square/Covent Garden*

🚌 *14, 19, 24, 29, 38, 176*

🚃 *Charing Cross*

Ⓟ *Upper St Martin's Lane/Shelton Street*

✱ *Air Condition*   ◁) *Infra-red*

♿ *Stalls*

☆ *Fine Art Deco architectural details*

When this theatre opened in 1930, the simplicity and modernity of its design by Wimperis, Simpson and Guthrie, with an interior by Serge Chermayeff, was much commented on. The exterior is of undecorated Portland stone, with the unusual corner entrance on Seven Dials rising to an open three sided loggia on its top storey which lies proud of the main building. The auditorium of painted concrete is spanned by plain acoustic arch ribs across the ceiling. There is a gold Art Deco mural of dancers above the doors between the inner and outer foyers, and another in the inner foyer. The diversity of productions it has housed beggars most other venues, with opera, ballet, classical drama, musicals, films and even ice and magic shows. It opened with Beatrice Lilly in the revue *Charlot's Masquerade*. Early visitors included the Comédie Française (1934) but it became a venue for trade film shows by the late 1930s. In 1946 the New London Opera Company was established, presenting its own revivals such as *Don Pasquale*, and visiting Italian and French companies. A return to drama saw the old school *Affairs Of State* (1952) and William Douglas Home's *The Reluctant Debutante* (1955), succeeded by contemporary drama with John Mortimer's first play *The Wrong Side Of The Park* (1960) and Albert Finney making his name as Keith Waterhouse and Willis Hall's *Billy Liar* (1960). Two big musical successes were Tommy Steele in *Half A Sixpence* (1963) and Bruce Forsyth in *Little Me* (1964). These were followed by the last gasp of operetta with John Hanson in *The Desert Song* and *The Student Prince* (1968). The National Theatre played a season here in 1970 with Maggie Smith in *Hedda Gabler* directed by Ingmar Bergman, and Laurence Olivier in *The Merchant Of Venice*. The Cambridge then entered a low period with a seemingly endless succession of musical flops. John Curry's *Theatre Of Skating* (1977) brought ice dancing to the West End and *The Magic Castle* (1984) a Las Vegas style magic show. After closure and refurbishment in 1987 it has been on a more even keel, with the D'Oyly Carte Opera Company launching a comeback with *Iolanthe* and *The Yeomen Of The Guard* (1988), and long runs of the musicals *Return To The Forbidden Planet* (1989), *Fame* (1995) and *Grease* (1996).

Cambridge Theatre

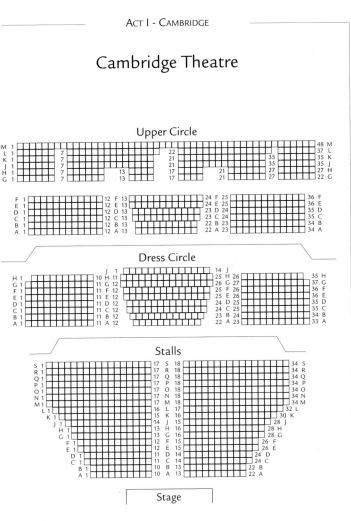

Upper Circle

Dress Circle

Stalls

Stage

64▲ Upper Circle, 31▲ Dress Circle, 5▼ Stalls, 0▲ Foyer, ♿ 1287

Coliseum

⌨ St Martin's Lane, WC2N 4ES

☎ 020 7632 8300

✍ www.eno.org

⊖ Leicester Square/Charing Cross

🚌 3, 6, 9, 11, 12, 13, 15, 23, 24, 29, 53, 77A, 88, 91, 159, 176

🚃 Charing Cross

Ⓟ Upper St Martin's Lane/Bedfordbury

↯ Infra-red

♿ Stalls

☆ The "revolving" globe on its tower is one of London's landmark sights

London's largest theatre, designed by Frank Matcham on the instruction of Oswald Stoll to be its grandest variety house, opened in 1904 as the London Coliseum. The Italian Renaissance exterior style is faced in terracotta, with balconied windows set in loggias on the second floor, surmounted by a tower with a globe on top. This globe originally revolved, but after a protracted dispute with the local council, it remained fixed with lights installed inside which give the impression of movement. Figures at the base of the tower represent Art, Music, Science and Literature. The lavishly decorated auditorium is unusual in that the circles do not overhang the stalls. Matcham's design employed the latest technology including the world's first revolving stage, in three concentric rings of 25ft, 50ft and 75ft diameter, capable of moving in either direction. This allowed the staging of horse and chariot races against the movement for the revolve among the theatre's many spectaculars. There were four shows daily at noon, 3pm, 6pm and 9pm, presenting two different programmes, so that patrons could see one, take tea on the roof and be entertained by a band in the hour-long interval, and then see the second. The initial expense was so great that the original company failed after two years. Stoll bought it back and reopened it successfully with all manner of attractions, including music hall stars, performing animals and circus acts, mixed with legitimate acts such as Ellen Terry performing excerpts from *The Merchant Of Venice*, Sarah Bernhardt, Lillie Langtry, and Diaghilev's Russian Ballet. The first public demonstration of television was staged here in 1930. The name was shortened to the Coliseum in 1931 when it became a regular theatre with the opening of *White Horse Inn*. It saw the London premieres of many of the great American shows such as *Annie Get Your Gun* (1947), *Kiss Me Kate* (1951), *Guys And Dolls* (1953), *Can Can* (1955), *The Pajama Game* (1955) and *Damn Yankees* (1957). Times changed, its size became a problem, and it was converted to a Cinerama cinema in 1963 before finally closing. Fortunately it staved off demolition and in 1968 the Coliseum became home to Sadler's Wells Opera, renamed English National Opera in 1974.

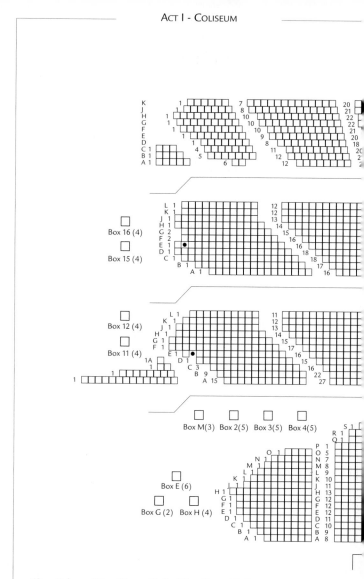

68▲ Balcony, 56▲ Upper Circle, 33▲ Dress Circle
2▼ Stalls, 0▲ Foyer, 🎟2,358

Coliseum

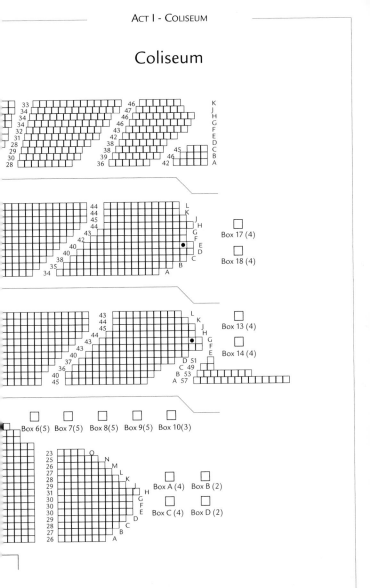

Comedy

⌨ *Panton Street, SW1Y 4DN*

☎ *020 7369 1731*

✎ *www.theambassadors.com*

⊖ *Piccadilly Circus / Leicester Square*

🚌 *3, 6, 9, 12, 13, 15, 23, 53, 88, 139, 159*

🚃 *Charing Cross*

Ⓟ *Whitcomb Street / Denman Street*

◀ *Infra-red*

♿ *Dress Circle*

☆ *Tiny but charming Royal Room with a fireplace in the vestibule*

The Comedy opened in 1881 as the Royal Comedy, but three years later the Royal was removed at the insistence of Buckingham Palace as no official warrant had been issued. Designed by Thomas Verity, the theatre has a pedimented classical façade with a Greek "lady with a lamp" statue in a blind window recess above the entrance. The Renaissance style auditorium was the oldest Victorian auditorium in London until a major refurbishment in 1954. Despite its modest size, the Comedy's original purpose was to present comic opera, and its opening production was *The Mascotte*, an opera comique by Audran. By the early years of the twentieth century however this had given way to drama, courtesy of Sir Frank Benson's company. Actors who have appeared at the Comedy include Herbert Beerbohm Tree, Sarah Bernhardt and Marie Tempest. John Barrymore gave his first London performance here in 1905 and it was here too that Gerald Du Maurier created the role of E W Hornung's *Raffles,* the gentleman burglar (1906). A few years later in 1914 Laurette Taylor had a great success here with *Peg O' My Heart* and throughout World Wars I and II the Comedy staged the revues of C B Cochrane and Andre Charlot. In 1956 it became home to the New Watergate Theatre Club, which was set up to produce plays which had been refused a licence by the Lord Chamberlain. It presented Arthur Miller's *A View From The Bridge* (1956) - the opening night of which was attended by Arthur Miller, Marilyn Monroe, Laurence Olivier and Vivien Leigh, Robert Anderson's *Tea And Sympathy* (1957), Tennessee Williams's *Cat On A Hot Tin Roof* (1958) and *Five Finger Exercise* (1958). The high profile support that these productions received helped liberalise attitudes in the censor's office. Since then the Comedy has seen the premieres of a number of other controversial plays including Peter Nichols' *A Day In The Death Of Joe Egg* (1967), *Fortune And Men's Eyes* (1968), David Hare's *Knuckle* (1974), Nell Dunn's *Steaming* (1980), and John Guarre's *Six Degrees Of Separation* (1993). It has also become known as the West End home of Harold Pinter's plays with productions of *The Homecoming* (1991), *The Caretaker* (1992 and 2000), *No Man's Land* (1993), *Moonlight* (1995) and *The Hothouse* (1995).

Comedy

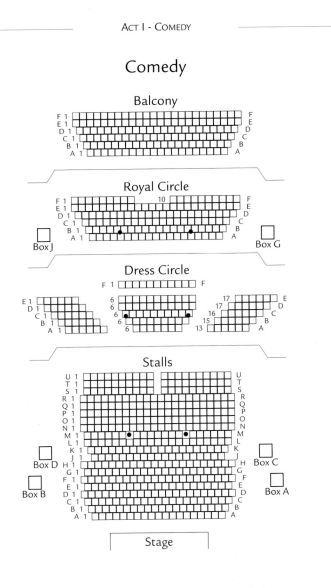

Balcony

Royal Circle

Box J   Box G

Dress Circle

Stalls

Box D   Box C

Box B   Box A

Stage

50▲ Balcony, 23▲ Upper Circle, 0▲ Dress Circle
24▾ Stalls, 2▲ Foyer, 🐾794

Criterion

- 🏠 *Piccadilly Circus, W1V 9LB*
- ☎ *020 7413 1437*
- ⊖ *Piccadilly Circus*
- 🚌 *3, 6, 9, 12, 13, 14, 15, 19, 22, 23, 38, 53, 88, 94, 139, 159*
- 🚆 *Charing Cross*
- ℗ *Denman Street/Whitcomb Street*
- ✈ *Air Condition*   ◁ *Induction Loop*
- ♿ *Upper Circle*
- ☆ *Unique tiling and mirrors in corridors and stairs*

In 1873 a large restaurant called the Criterion was built on the south side of what was then Regent Circus, on the site of the White Bear, a two hundred year old post inn. A small concert hall was planned for the centre of the building, but at the last minute this was changed to a theatre which duly opened in 1874. Thomas Verity was responsible for the design, which was unique in that it was entirely underground, requiring air to be continuously pumped into it, with only the box office at street level. The classical stone façade is in the second Empire manner while inside the stairs and corridors leading to the bars and auditorium have gilded mirrors and are elaborately tiled with paintings of classical figures and the names of great composers (from when it was to be a concert hall). Initially the theatre was not an unqualified success and in an effort to make it feel less claustrophobic Verity remodelled it in 1883, extending the public areas, and introducing electric lighting and air conditioning for the first time. The final result is considered by some to be the most beautiful theatre in London, with ornate pink and white wedding cake style decoration in the auditorium. From the outset it was established as a home for comedy. Among the great names that have appeared are Mary Moore, Charles Hawtrey, Sybil Thorndyke and Marie Tempest. It has been the launchpad of many careers, witnessing John Gielgud's debut in *Musical Chairs* (1932) and Terence Rattigan's first big success *French Without Tears* (1936). Because of its underground situation the theatre was taken over by the BBC as a radio studio during World War II, and many variety programmes including ITMA were broadcast from here. Theatre returned with Edith Evans in *The Rivals* (1945), Samuel Beckett's *Waiting For Godot* (1955), and Jean Anouilh's *The Waltz Of The Toreadors* (1956), both directed by Peter Hall, transferred here from the Arts Theatre Club. The theatre closed in the late 1980s while the building surrounding it and the adjoining restaurant were demolished and reconstructed, retaining their original façade. Luckily the Criterion emerged not only unscathed but restored, reopening in 1992. The Reduced Shakespeare Company in the *Complete Works Of Shakespeare* (Abridged) has become its longest running show.

Criterion

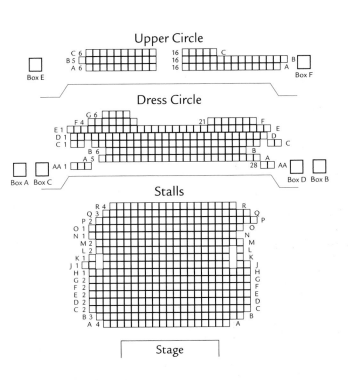

Upper Circle

C 6
B 5
A 6
Box E

16   C
16
16   A   B
Box F

Dress Circle

G 6
F 4
E 1
D 1
C 1
B 6
A 5
AA 1
Box A   Box C

21   F
E
D
C
B
28   A   AA
Box D   Box B

Stalls

R 4   R
Q 3   Q
P 2   P
O 1   O
N 1   N
M 2   M
L 2   L
K 1   K
J 1   J
H   H
G 2   G
F 2   F
E 2   E
D 2   D
C 2   C
B 3   B
A 4   A

Stage

26▼ +10▲ Upper Circle, 32▼ Dress Circle,
51▼ Stalls, 1▲ Foyer, 🦻 598

51

Dominion

- ⌨ *Tottenham Court Road, W1P 0AQ*
- ☎ *0870 607 7460*
- 🖋 *www.apollo-leisure.co.uk*
- ⊖ *Tottenham Court Road*
- 🚌 *1, 7, 8, 10, 14, 19, 24, 25, 29, 38, 55, 73, 98, 134, 176, 242*
- 🚆 *Charing Cross*
- ℗ *Great Russell Street/Museum Street*
- ♿ *Stalls Using Stairlift*
- ☆ *Grand mirrored foyer with mezzanine*

This site has variously housed the St Giles Leper Hospital (founded 1101), the Meux brewery (where a twenty two foot high vat of porter ale burst in 1814 drowning eight people), the Court cinema (built 1911), O'Brien's Fun Fair, and finally Luna Park, a venue for thrice daily variety shows. The present building was designed by the brothers William and T R Millburn to operate as both a theatre and cinema and opened in 1929. Although it occupies a whole block, there is only a narrow street frontage with a Portland stone façade in late French Renaissance style, which has recently re-emerged from behind a hoarding. Inside circulation space is generous with twin staircases to a mezzanine, where there was originally a café over the entrance. This leads to a cavernous auditorium graced with the simple lines of a neo-Renaissance picture palace of the 1930s. If the Upper Circle were to be restored it would have 2835 seats, making it the largest theatre in London. Although it opened with the de Sylva, Henderson and Brown stage musical *Follow Through*, starring Elsie Randolph, Ivy Tresmand and Leslie Henson, the Dominion has for most of its life, functioned as a super cinema with occasional concerts, and short opera and ballet seasons. During this time a number of prestige films received their first London showing here, beginning with Lon Chaney's sound version of *The Phantom Of The Opera* (1930), and Charlie Chaplin's *City Lights* (1931). In 1958 a huge Todd AO screen and new projection box were installed and the Upper Circle closed off. At that time films enjoyed runs of several years which seem unthinkable today, *South Pacific* (1958-62), *West Side Story* (1962-65), and *The Sound Of Music* (1965-73). Films then alternated with concerts and visits from regional and international opera and ballet companies until 1981 when it reverted to live shows only. The Dominion returned to mainstream theatre use in 1986 with probably the worst example of the '80s mega musical in Dave Clark's *Time*. Following that it was under serious threat of redevelopment which was finally ended and a modest refurbishment carried out. Shows since then have spanned the good: *Grand Hotel* (1992), the bad: *Bernadette* (1990) and the ugly: *Notre-Dame de Paris* (2000). The most successful were *Grease* (1993) and *Disney's Beauty And The Beast* (1996).

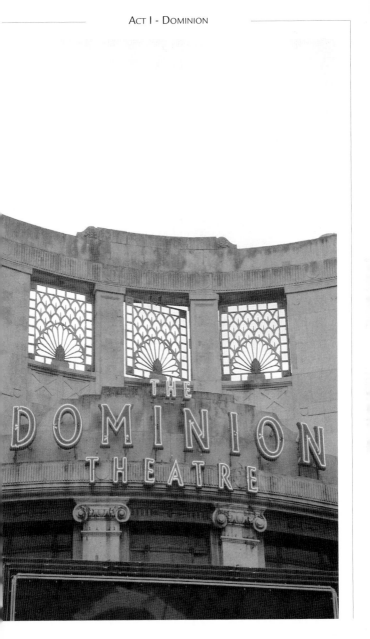

53

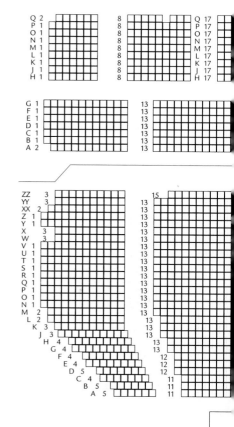

32 ▲ Dress Circle,
10 ▲ Stalls, 0 ▲ Foyer, 🏛 2182

Dominion

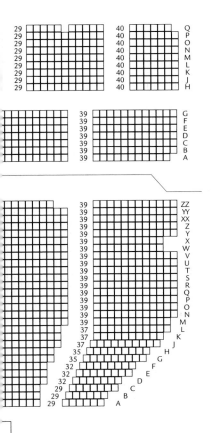

Donmar Warehouse

⌸ *Thomas Neal's, Earlham Street, WC2H 9LD*
☏ *020 7369 1732*
✎ *www.donmar-warehouse.co.uk*
⊖ *Leicester Square/Covent Garden*
🚌 *14, 19, 24, 29, 38, 176*
🚃 *Charing Cross*
Ⓟ *Shelton Street/Upper St Martin's Lane*
✈ *Air Condition*   ⦚ *Infra-red*
♿ *Stalls Lift available*
☆ *The West End's only Off Broadway style thrust stage theatre*

Boston Marriage

The building was originally constructed in the 1870s as the vat room of a brewery, which in 1920 became a film studio – the first in Britain to use colour – before returning to commercial use as a fruit warehouse. The theatre takes its name from a theatre lighting hire company which was once based here, whose name in turn was made up from two names Don(ald) and Mar(got). The Donald in question was Donald Albery the theatre owner, and the Margot, ballerina Margot Fonteyn. They formed a company to produce a ballet season, and when it ended Albery started hiring out the equipment it had purchased. The auditorium was originally used as a rehearsal room, but when the Royal Shakespeare Company was looking for a London space to show productions from its Stratford studio The Other Place, in 1977 a new theatre The Warehouse was born. Despite its cramped and makeshift facilities it rapidly became a very popular venue, staging, amongst others, the original productions of *Piaf* and *Educating Rita*. When the RSC moved to the Barbican in 1981 it was reborn as the Donmar Warehouse. London finally had the

Donmar Warehouse

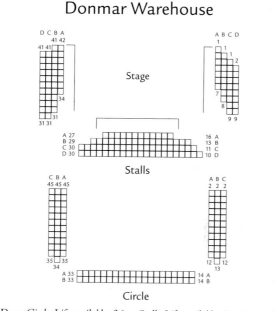

Stage

Stalls

Circle

48 ▲ Dress Circle Lift available, 26 ▲ Stalls Lift available, 0 – Foyer, ♿252

equivalent of an Off Broadway theatre – an independent venue available for hire to small producers at a reasonable price. A wide range of work could be seen here and the opportunity was created for touring companies to present their shows in London. Particularly successful were the Show People seasons devoted to the work of American musical theatre writers. The Donmar was then closed and refurbished when the block in which it is located was redeveloped. This brought a layer of designer chic to the previous exposed brickwork, egalitarian bench seating and better technical facilities, but sacrificed some of the rough and ready charm of the place. It reopened in 1992 as a producing venue of limited runs under the direction of the then little known Sam Mendes. Since then a number of landmark productions have transferred to other West End theatres for extended runs and also Broadway. These include Kander and Ebb's *Cabaret* (1993), Noel Coward's *Design For Living* (1994), Stephen Sondheim's *Company* (1995), Sophocles' *Electra* (1997), Tom Stoppard's *The Real Thing* (1999) and, most sensationally, Nicole Kidman and Iain Glen in *The Blue Room* (1998).

Theatre Royal Drury Lane

⌨ *Catherine Street WC2B 5JF*

☎ *020 7494 5000*

✎ *www.rutheatres.com*

⊖ *Covent Garden / Holborn / Temple*

🚌 *1, 4, 6, 9, 11, 13, 15, 23, 26, 59, 68, 76, 77A, 91, 168, 171, 172*

🚃 *Charing Cross*

Ⓟ *Drury Lane / Shelton Street*

✹ *Air Condition*   ⌁ *Infra-red*

♿ *Stalls*

☆ *The Rotunda and Dress Circle Grand Saloon, and a large collection of paintings, statues and busts throughout the building*

This is the oldest site in the world in continuous theatrical use. The first theatre was constructed in 1663 to house The King's Servants, one of only two theatre companies granted a royal charter or Patent allowing them to perform plays, after the restoration of Charles II. The entire theatre was the size of the present stage. After it was destroyed by fire, Christopher Wren designed a second building, more than twice the size of the first, which opened in 1674. The fourth and present building, was designed in 1812 by Benjamin Wyatt. Samuel Beazley added the portico in 1820 and the Russell Street colonnade in 1831. The original splendour of the grand staircase, rotunda and saloon are not quite matched by the auditorium redesigned by Emblin Walker, Robert Crombie and Frederick Jones in 1922. This is in Empire style with three large boxes framed by pilasters with columns of imitation lapis lazuli with gilt capitals, and a panelled ceiling with multiple pendant fittings. Most of the greatest British actors have played here, including Nell Gwynne, David Garrick, Henry Irving, Edmund Kean, John Philip Kemble, William Charles Macready, Mrs Siddons, Ellen Terry, Dan Leno and the clown Grimaldi. *Sheridan's School For Scandal* received its premiere in 1777; Kings George I and III both survived assassination attempts at the theatre; ironically it was here too that *God Save The King* was first sung in 1741 and *Rule Britannia* in 1750. It has staged every form of entertainment from Shakespeare through melodrama and opera to pantomime with grand Victorian spectacles offering sinking ships, chariot races, erupting volcanoes, and earthquakes thrown in for good measure. Noel Coward's *Cavalcade* (1931) featured a cast and crew of over 300. Among Ivor Novello's shows *Glamorous Night* (1935) boasted a liner on fire which sank, *Careless Rapture* (1936) Hampstead Heath with Bank Holiday fairground roundabouts, and *Crest Of The Wave* (1937) a train crash. During World War II it housed the forces' entertainment organisation ENSA. Since then shows have included Rogers and Hammerstein's *Oklahoma!* (1947), *Carousel* (1950), *South Pacific*

(1951) and *The King And I* (1953), Lerner and Lowe's *My Fair Lady* (1958 and 2001) and *Camelot* (1964), *Hello, Dolly!* (1965), *A Chorus Line* (1976), *42nd Street* (1984), and *Miss Saigon* (1989). It is arguably the most famous theatre in the world.

Theatre Royal Drury Lane

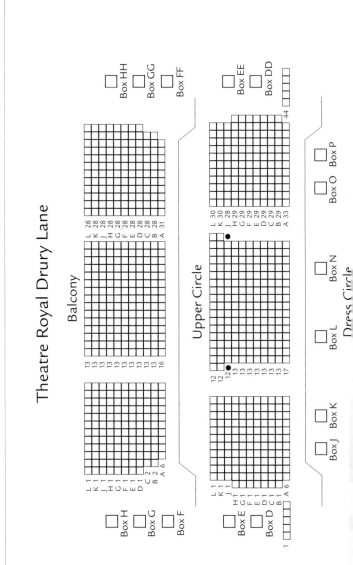

Theatre Royal Drury Lane

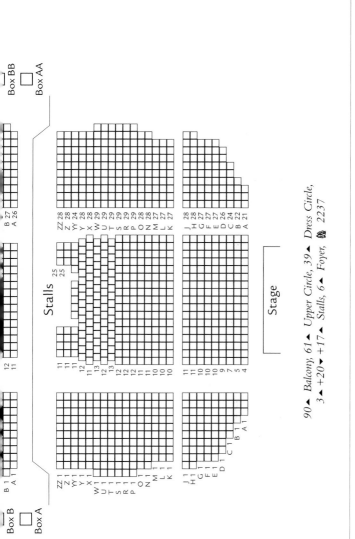

Duchess

- ⌨ *Catherine Street, WC2B 5LA*
- ☏ *020 7494 5075*
- ✎ *www.rutheatres.com*
- ⊖ *Covent Garden/Holborn/Temple*
- 🚌 *1, 4, 6, 9, 11, 13, 15, 76, 168, 171, 172, 176, 188, 243, 341*
- 🚉 *Charing Cross*
- Ⓟ *Drury Lane/Shelton Street*
- ✈ *Air Condition* ◁ *Infra-red*
- ☆ *One of the West End's most intimate theatres*

Duchess

The Duchess was designed by Ewen Barr and opened in 1929. The awkward nature of the site means that the circle is narrower than the stalls, the foyer and box office are tucked under the circle, and the dressing rooms are stacked onto the auditorium. The modern Tudor Gothic style stone exterior has three bays of windows with enamelled panels containing relief insignia between the floors. The interior by French designers Marc-Henri Levy and Gaston Laverdet was created to avoid visible light fittings and so recessed fixtures provide reflected illumination. The auditorium is fan shaped in a very plain 'moulded' style, the only decoration being a pair of bas-relief panels of figures holding masks above applauding hands by Maurice Lambert between the proscenium and the circle. On the stairs and in the corridors illuminated glass fronted niches were created to contain works of art – nowadays sadly replaced by merchandise. The Duchess holds the record for London's shortest run with *The Intimate Revue* (1930) which failed to reach the end of its first night. Everything that could go wrong did so, creating long gaps between scenes and by midnight, with seven more scenes to go, they cut to the finale – and the next day cancelled the run. Following a production of his play *Laburnum Grove* (1933) J B Priestley became associated with the management and *Eden End* (1934), *Cornelius* (1935), *Time And The Conways* (1937) and *The Linden Tree* (1947) premiered here. Emlyn Williams, who had appeared in the opening production *Tunnel Trench*, returned in *Night Must Fall* (1935) which established him as a writer, and *The Corn Is Green* (1938) with Sybil Thorndyke. T S Eliot's *Murder In The Cathedral* (1936) made its West End debut here, as did Terence Rattigan's *The Deep Blue Sea* (1952) with Peggy Ashcroft and Kenneth More, and Harold Pinter's *The Caretaker* (1960), *The Basement and The Tea Party* (1970) and *Other Places* (1985). It has seen many transfers from other theatres including Noel Coward's *Blithe Spirit* (1942) which ran for 1997 performances (London's longest run before *The Mousetrap*), Bill Naughton's *Alfie* (1963), *Oh! Calcutta* (1974) which ran for six years, *No Sex Please We're British* (1986), and *Don't Dress For Dinner* (1992).

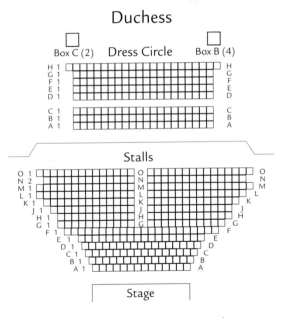

Duchess

Box C (2)   Dress Circle   Box B (4)

Stalls

Stage

12 ▲ Dress Circle, 21 ▼ Stalls, 1 ▲ Foyer, 476

Duke Of York's

⌨ *St Martin's Lane, WC2N 4BG*
☎ *020 7369 1791*
🖳 *www.theambassadors.com*
☉ *Charing Cross/Leicester Square*
🚌 *3, 6, 9, 11, 12, 13, 15, 23, 24, 29, 53, 77A, 88, 91, 159, 176*
🚆 *Charing Cross*
Ⓟ *Bedfordbury/Upper St Martin's Lane*
◀ *Infra-red*
♿ *Dress Circle*
☆ *Dress Circle bar offers access to first floor loggia*

Opening in 1892 as the Trafalgar Square Theatre, it was designed by Walter Emden with the novelty of real open fires in the auditorium. The name was changed to the Duke Of York's in 1895 to honour the future King George V. The exterior is of painted brick and stone with a small central open loggia at first floor level. Owing to the restricted width of the site the auditorium is narrow and deep and supporting pillars originally created a large number of restricted view seats. These pillars were removed in a major refurbishment in 1979 that restored the original decorative scheme of cream, gold and russet. Unusually there is no formal proscenium arch, the stage opening simply being defined by the pillars supporting the stage boxes. Among the audiences to have seen David Belasco's one act curtain-raiser *Madame Butterfly* (1900) was Puccini, who was inspired to write his opera of the same name. J M Barrie had a long association with the theatre, which started with *The Admirable Crichton* (1902). This was a success despite a strike by the stage staff on the first night, with the result that the cast, which included Gerald du Maurier, had to move the scenery themselves. Peter Pan made his stage debut here in 1904 and returned every Christmas until 1914, with Noel Coward playing Slightly Soiled in 1912. Other Barrie plays produced here were *What Every Woman Knows* (1908), *Old Friends*, *The Twelve Pound Look* and *Rosalind*. Coward returned to premiere the revues *London Calling* (1923) with Gertrude Lawrence, *Easy Virtue* (1926), *Home Chat* (1927) and *Waiting In The Wings* (1960). Other important plays to receive their first performances here were Henrik Ibsen's *The Master Builder* and George Bernard Shaw's *Misalliance*. The actor's union Equity was formed as a result of a meeting held here by a group of actors in 1920. Landmark productions of more recent years include Orson Welles's *Moby Dick* (1955), Frank Marcus's *The Killing Of Sister George* (1965), Alan Ayckbourn's first major success *Relatively Speaking* (1967) and Richard Harris's *Stepping Out* (1984). A long association with the Royal Court Theatre has seen many transfers, including Ariel Dorfman's *Death And The Maiden* (1992), and David Mamet's *Oleanna* (1993).

Duke of York's

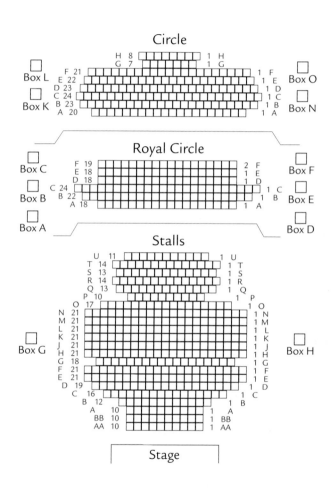

Circle

Box L
Box K

H 8   1 H
G 7   1 G
F 21   1 F
E 22   1 E
D 23   1 D
C 24   1 C
B 23   1 B
A 20

Box O
Box N

Royal Circle

Box C
Box B
Box A

F 19   2 F
E 18   1 E
D 18   1 D
C 24   1 C
B 22   1 B
A 18   1 A

Box F
Box E
Box D

Stalls

Box G

U 11   1 U
T 14   1 T
S 13   1 S
R 14   1 R
Q 13   1 Q
P 10   1 P
O 17   1 O
N 21   1 N
M 21   1 M
L 21   1 L
K 21   1 K
J 21   1 J
H   1 H
G   1 G
F 21   1 F
E 21   1 E
D 19   1 D
C 16   1 C
B 12   1 B
A 10   1 A
BB 10   1 BB
AA 10   1 AA

Box H

Stage

23▲ Upper Circle, 0▲ Dress Circle, 20▼ Stalls, 0▲ Foyer, 🎭 650

65

Fortune

⌨ *Russell Street, WC2B 5HH*

☎ *020 7836 2238*

⊖ *Covent Garden/Holborn/Temple*

🚌 *1, 4, 6, 9, 11, 68, 76, 77A, 91, 168, 171, 172, 176, 188, 243, 341*

🚃 *Charing Cross*

℗ *Drury Lane/Shelton Street*

✈ *Air Condition*

☆ *The most intimate West End theatre almost feels like a private house*

The first West End theatre to be built after World War I stands on the site of the Albion Tavern, a haunt of Georgian and Victorian actors and writers. It was originally to be called the Crown as it is 'grafted onto' the Scottish National Church in Crown Court, with an entrance passageway passing through its entire depth on the left hand side, and the church hall beneath it. The opening production was appropriately (or inappropriately) a play called *Sinners*. Designed by Ernest Schaufelberg in 1924 it is a radical departure from previous theatres, without fully embracing the Art Deco style of those that came soon after. It is a plain square building of brick and stucco, its windows giving a hint of the Medieval, the only external decoration being a statue of Fortune high above the entrance – although this is claimed to be Terpsichore the Greek Muse of dancing by some. Original ornamental doors give way to the marble and copper foyer with a brass plate bearing the Shakespearean inscription "There is a tide in the affairs of men which, taken at the flood, leads on to Fortune". The auditorium is remarkably intimate, containing about the same number of seats as the balcony of Drury Lane whose stage door it faces. The restricted size of both the stage and the auditorium has dictated the shows it has presented. Its early days saw a number of undistinguished plays, with Frederick Lonsdale's *On Approval* (1927) its first success. The People's National Theatre run by Nancy Price established itself here in 1930, presenting John Galsworthy's first play *The Silver Box* (1931). During World War II it was taken over by the services' entertainment organisation ENSA which was based in Drury Lane. After the war, *Power Without Glory* (1947) brought two unknowns, Dirk Bogarde and Kenneth More, to the West End. Two revues, Michael Flanders and Donald Swan's *At The Drop Of A Hat* (1957) and *Beyond The Fringe* (1961) with Alan Bennett, Peter Cook, Jonathan Miller and Dudley Moore, defined the times in which they were presented. Long running transfers of Peter Shaffer's *Sleuth* (1973), Vivian Ells's *Mr Cinders* (1983) and Susan Hill's *The Woman In Black* (1990) have also been important in their genres.

Fortune

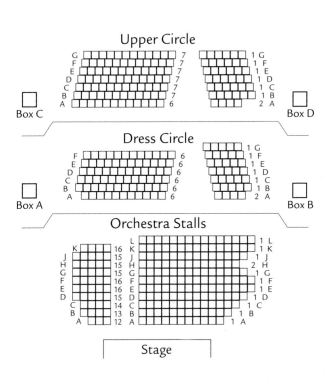

Upper Circle

G
F
E
D
C
B
A
7
7
7
7
7
7
6

1 G
1 F
1 E
1 D
1 C
1 B
2 A

Box C

Box D

Dress Circle

F
E
D
C
B
A
6
6
6
6
6
6

1 G
1 F
1 E
1 D
1 C
1 B
2 A

Box A

Box B

Orchestra Stalls

K
J
H
G
F
E
D
C
B
A
16
15
15
15
16
16
15
14
13
12

L
K
J
H
G
F
E
D
C
B
A

1 L
1 K
1 J
2 H
1 G
1 F
1 D
1 C
1 B
1 A

Stage

45▲ Upper Circle, 7▲ Dress Circle, 21▼ Stalls, 0▲ Foyer, ♿ 440

67

Garrick

⌨ *Charing Cross Road, WC2H 0HH*

☎ *020 7494 5085*

✍ *www.rutheatres.com*

☻ *Leicester Square / Charing Cross*

🚌 *3, 6, 9, 11, 12, 13, 15, 23, 24, 29, 53, 77A, 88, 91, 159, 176*

🚉 *Charing Cross* Ⓟ *Bedfordbury / Lisle Street*

↙ *Infra-red*

♿ *Dress Circle*

☆ *A copy of a lost Gainsborough portrait of the actor manager David Garrick adorns the wood panelled foyer bar*

The building was financed by W S Gilbert – of 'and Sullivan' fame – and designed by Walter Emden, with contributions by C J Phipps. Construction was almost abandoned half-way through when excavations uncovered an underground river. Gilbert is said to have remarked that he did not know "whether to go on with the building or let the fishing rights". It was the first British theatre to be named after an actor. The distinctive curved Portland and Bath stone frontage incorporates a colonnaded loggia at first floor level that can be reached via the Dress Circle bar. The auditorium is decorated in Italian Renaissance style in cream and red, with Cupids holding laurel decked shields decorating the plasterwork on the balcony fronts. As at the Duke of York's there is no formal proscenium arch, the stage opening simply being defined by the supporting pillars of the stage boxes. The Garrick eventually opened in 1889 with Pinero's *The Profligate*, followed by his *Lady Bountiful* (1891), *The Notorious Mrs Ebbsmith* (1895), and *Iris* (1901) and it has mostly been associated with comedies. In 1934 an unsuccessful attempt was made to revive Old Time Music Hall and shortly after this plans were announced for its rebuilding as a super cinema but the scheme never materialised. Walter Greenwood's *Love On The Dole* (1935) was a great success that established both the theatre and Wendy Hiller its star. In the 1940s ex Aldwych farceurs – performers Robertson Hare and Robert Drayton, and writers Vernon Sylvane and Ben Travers – moved in with *Warn That Man (1941)*, *Aren't Men Beasts* (1942), *She Follows Me About* (1943) and *Madame Louise (1945)*. After the World War II Jack Buchanan assumed direction of the theatre, appearing in Frederick Lonsdale's *Canaries Sometimes Sing* (1947), and Sylvanes's *As Long As They're Happy* (1953). He also presented Yolanda Donlan in Garson Kanin's *Born Yesterday* (1947) directed by Laurence Olivier, and *To Dorothy A Son* (1951). In 1967 Brian Rix moved his company here from the Whitehall with farces such as *Stand By Your Bedouin* and *Don't Just Lie There Say Something*. *No Sex Please We're British* (1982) transferred for a four year run, the theatre's longest until the transfer of the National Theatre production of J B Priestley's *An Inspector Calls* (1995).

Garrick

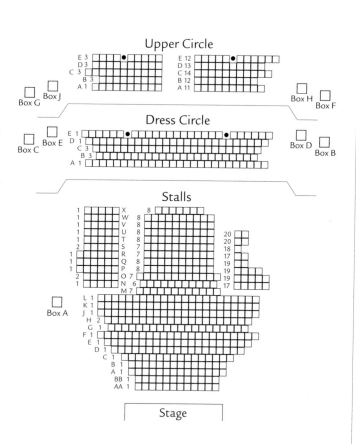

Upper Circle

E 3
D 3
C 3
B 3
A 1

E 12
D 13
C 14
B 12
A 11

Box G   Box J

Box H   Box F

Dress Circle

E 1
D 1
C 3
B 3
A 1

Box C   Box E

Box D   Box B

Stalls

1
1
1
1
1
2
1
1
1
2
1

X
W
V
U
T
S
R
Q
P
O
N
M

8
8
8
8
8
7
8
8
7
6
7

20
20
18
17
19
19
19
17

L 1
K 1
J 1
H 2
G 1
F 1
E 1
D 1
C 1
B 1
A 1
BB 1
AA 1

Box A

Stage

25▲ +8▼ Upper Circle, 0▲ Dress Circle, 29▼ Stalls, 2▲ Foyer, ♿ 656

69

Gielgud

⌨ *Shaftesbury Avenue, W1V 8AR*
☏ *020 7494 5065*
✉ *www.rutheatres.com*
⊖ *Piccadilly Circus*
🚌 *14, 19, 38*
🚃 *Charing Cross*
Ⓟ *Brewer Street/Denman Street*
✈ *Air Condition*   ◁ᐟ *Infra-red*
♿ *Dress Circle*
☆ *A bust of John Gielgud in the Foyer*

Designed by W G R Sprague the Hicks Theatre opened in 1906, but was known as the Globe from 1909, before becoming the Gielgud in 1994. Like the Strand and the Aldwych, also designed by Sprague, it bookends a whole block with the Queen's Theatre. The four storey Edwardian Baroque façade in Portland stone surmounted by a domed turret makes the most of its corner site. The Dress Circle bar, reached by a Regency staircase, has an oval gallery from which patrons can look down on the foyer, as at the Aldwych. The auditorium is in Louis XVI style, with Corinthian columns framing the boxes and an allegorical cartouche above the proscenium. Actor manager Seymour Hicks, built and named the theatre, and he, together with his wife Ellaline Terriss, appeared in the opening production, a musical play *The Beauty Of Bath,* which transferred from the Aldwych. Star names, often in not very distinguished plays or comedies, and starladen revivals have been its staple fare. The management of actress Marie Lohr and husband Anthony Prinsep raised the standards with Somerset Maugham's *Our Betters* (1923), Frederick Lonsdale's *Aren't We All?* (1923) and Noel Coward's *Fallen Angels* (1925). Probably its heyday came when the H M Tennant management established its headquarters in the building, producing a succession of classic revivals both in house and at other theatres. The first were George Bernard Shaw's *Candida* (1937), Somerset Maughan's *The Constant Wife* (1937) with Ruth Chatterton making her London debut, and the landmark production of Oscar Wilde's *The Importance Of Being Earnest* (1939), directed by and starring John Gielgud, with Edith Evans giving the definitive performance as Lady Bracknell. Important new plays were Christopher Fry's *The Lady's Not For Burning* (1949), Fry's translation of Jean Anouilh's *Ring Round The Moon* with Paul Schofield as good and bad twins, Noel Coward's *Nude With Violin* (1956), and Robert Bolt's *A Man For All Seasons* (1960), also starring Paul Schofield. Many of Alan Ayckbourn's plays had their London premiere here: *The Norman Conquests* trilogy starring Tom Courtenay (1974), *Ten Times Table* (1978), *Man Of The Moment* (1989), *Communicating Doors* (1995) and *Things We Do For Love* (1998).

Gielgud

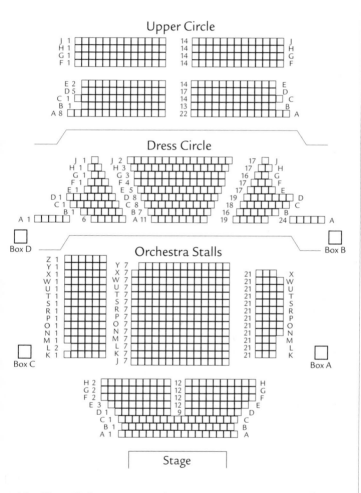

Upper Circle

Dress Circle

Box D

Box B

Orchestra Stalls

Box C

Box A

Stage

35 ▲ Upper Circle, 3 ▲ Dress Circle, 3 ▲ + 22 ▼ Stalls, 1 ▲ Foyer, ♿ 888

71

Theatre Royal Haymarket

🖾 *Haymarket, SW1Y 4HT*
☎ *020 7930 8800*
🖎 *www.trh.co.uk*
⊖ *Charing Cross/Piccadilly Circus*
🚌 *3, 6, 9, 12, 13, 15, 23, 53, 88, 139, 159*
🚃 *Charing Cross*
Ⓟ *Trafalgar Square/Whitcomb Street*
✷ *Air Condition*
♿ *Stalls*
☆ *The elegant mirrored vestibule at rear of the Dress Circle*

The Little Theatre In The Hay opened without a license in 1720 on a site adjoining the present building, and continued in this manner when a group of actors who broke away from the Drury Lane company, calling themselves 'The Comedians Of His Majesty's Revels' took it over. The crude satires performed under the management of Henry Fielding resulted in the introduction of theatre censorship in 1737. Eventually in 1766 under the management of Samuel Foote it became the third theatre to be granted a royal charter. The rumbustious nature of theatre-going in earlier times is demonstrated by two incidents which took place here. At a Royal Command performance in 1794 the crowd was so great that 15 people were crushed to death in a stampede. In 1805 the Tailors Riot occurred when hundreds of tailors, enraged by a satire on their trade, barracked a performance and troops were called to disperse them. The present building designed by John Nash, in classical style stucco with a Corinthian portico was constructed in 1821, and opened with Sheridan's *The Rivals*. The interior was remodelled in 1880 by C J Phipps, creating the first proscenium arch in the form of a four sided gold picture frame, and again in 1905 by C Stanley Peach in an elaborate Louis XVI style, restored in 1994. The name Theatre Royal Haymarket was assumed in 1855. Between 1853 and 1878 John Buckstone, probably the greatest theatre manager ever, presented more than 150 productions. Actor manager Herbert Beerbohm Tree took over in 1887, *Hamlet* and *Trilby* (1895), were so successful that he built Her Majesty's theatre opposite from the profits. Among plays to premiere here were Oscar Wilde's *A Woman Of No Importance* (1893) and Ibsen's *Ghosts* (1914). During World War II an H M Tennant/John Gielgud repertory season was presented with *Hamlet, A Midsummer Night's Dream, Love For Love, The Duchess Of Malfi* and *The Circle*. In recent times, successful productions of star names in classic revivals, Peter O'Toole in *Man And Superman* (1982) Lauren Bacall in *Sweet Bird Of Youth* (1985) and Jessica Lange in *A Streetcar Named Desire* (1997), have alternated with new plays making fast exits.

Theatre Royal Haymarket

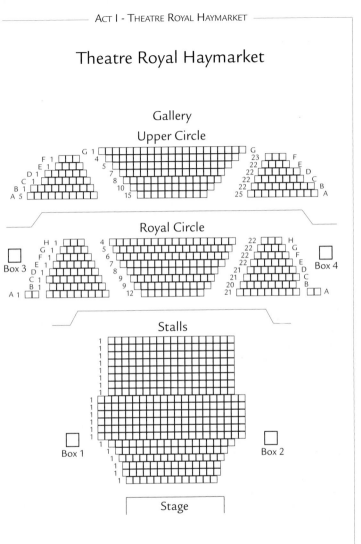

Gallery

Upper Circle

Royal Circle

Stalls

Box 3

Box 4

Box 1

Box 2

Stage

64▲ Upper Circle, 28▲ Dress Circle, 20▼ +11▲ Stalls, 3▲ Foyer, ♿888

Her Majesty's

⌨ *Haymarket, SW1Y 4QR*

☎ *020 7494 5400*

✍ *www.rutheatres.com*

⊖ *Charing Cross/Piccadilly Circus*

🚌 *3, 6, 9, 12, 13, 15, 23, 53, 88, 139, 159*

🚃 *Charing Cross*

Ⓟ *Trafalgar Square/Whitcomb Street*

✈ *Air Condition* ◁ *Infra-red*

♿ *Stalls*

☆ *The panelled foyer with a carved and painted ceiling*

The first theatre on this site, designed by John Vanburgh to house a company formed by William Congreve, opened in 1705 as the Queen's. After Handel staged his first opera in England, *Rinaldo* (1711), he received Royal patronage to establish a company, and it became the first theatre devoted entirely to Italian opera. Despite staging the first oratorio in England and other Handel operas it was not financially successful. The second theatre opened as the King's in 1791, and continued to present Italian opera and romantic ballet, changing its name to Her Majesty's Theatre, Italian Opera House in 1837, before dropping the Italian Opera House a decade later. English premieres included Mozart's *Cosi Fan Tutte* (1811), *The Magic Flute* (1811), *The Marriage Of Figaro* (1812) and *Don Giovanni* (1817), Beethoven's *Fidelio* (1851), Gounod's *Faust* (1863), Bizet's *Carmen* (1878) and the complete cycle of Wagner's *The Ring* (1882). After a further fire in 1867 a third theatre was reconstructed within the shell, but it was never really successful, offering a rag bag of opera, drama, revivalist meetings, pantomimes, and even boxing. The current building designed by C J Phipps for actor manager Herbert Beerbohm Tree opened in 1897. The façade is in French Renaissance Second Empire style of Portland stone, with a first floor loggia, and crowned with a copper clad dome. The interior is Louis XV style, with an auditorium inspired by Gabriel's opera house at Versailles, containing marble Corinthian columns and a painted ceiling, and featuring the first flat stage floor in Britain. Between 1897 and 1914 Tree staged eighteen sumptuous Shakespeare productions, and played Higgins to Mrs Patrick Campbell's Eliza in the premiere of George Bernard Shaw's *Pygmalion* (1914). In 1904 Tree started a drama school in the suite of rooms in the dome, which eventually became the Royal Academy of Dramatic Art, moving in 1905 to its present home in Gower Street. An abrupt change of management brought in the musical *Chu Chin Chow* (1916) whose record five year run remained unchallenged for nearly forty years. Since World War II Her Majesty's has presented a succession of great musicals, including *Brigadoon* (1949), *Paint Your Wagon* (1953), *West Side Story* (1958), *Fiddler On The Roof* (1967), and *The Phantom Of The Opera* (1986).

Her Majesty's

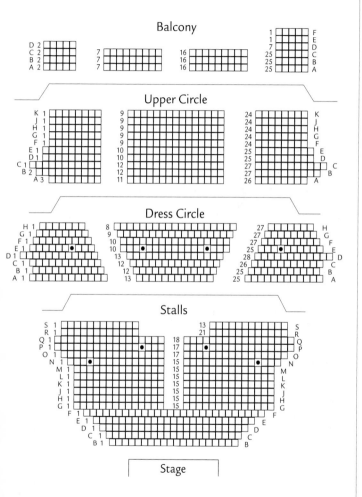

Balcony

Upper Circle

Dress Circle

Stalls

Stage

89▲ Balcony, 62▲ Upper Circle, 32▲ Dress Circle, 22▼ +18▲ Stalls,
0▲ Foyer, ♿1219

London Palladium

⌨ *Argyll Street, W1V 1AD*

☎ *020 7494 5020*

✉ *www.rutheatres.com*

⊖ *Oxford Circus*

🚌 *13, 15, 23, 25, 53, 55, 73, 88, 94, 98, 113, 139, 159, 176, C2*

🚆 *Charing Cross*

Ⓟ *Kingley Street/Poland Street*

✈ *Air Condition*   ◁) *Infra-red*

♿ *Stalls*

☆ *The Dress Circle bar contains a fountain*

Entertainment first came to this site in 1871 with the opening of Hengler's Grand Cirque, which was successful enough for a new enlarged building designed by C J Phipps to be constructed in 1884. When Hengler died soon after however it went into decline, and in 1895 became the National Ice Skating Palace. It was replaced in 1910 by the present building designed as a music hall by Frank Matcham, but retaining the Phipps portico. This was the height of the music hall boom and the owner Walter Gibbons wanted to out do rivals Oswald Stoll's Coliseum and Edward Moss's Hippodrome, both designed by Matcham. The richly furnished and gilded auditorium in French Rococo style, with a wide sweep of seats on three levels provided a capacity second only to the Coliseum and was unencumbered by pillars. At the rear of the stalls the Palm Court could serve one thousand people tea between performances while a ladies' orchestra played. The twice nightly programmes (plus three matinées) changed weekly and often included farce, melodrama, and opera excerpts, as well as variety turns, plus personal appearances by famous figures of the time. The same formula was used in *Sunday Night At The London Palladium*, the hour long live top rating television broadcasts that ran in the 1950s and 1960s, bringing the Palladium to its widest audience. In the 1920s the original format gave way to long running spectacular revues, and annual pantomimes which often ran until Easter. It earned the sobriquet "the world's greatest variety theatre" and has staged more Royal Variety Performances than any other. In 1932 a one off 'crazy week' developed into the Crazy Gang shows, featuring three double acts, Flanagan and Allen, Naughton and Gold, Nervo and Knox. After World War II many American stars made their London debuts here including Judy Garland, Bob Hope, Danny Kaye, Liberace, Ethel Merman and Frank Sinatra. In recent years it has become a home for musicals, including *The King And I* (1979 and 2000), Michael Crawford in *Barnum* (1981), Tommy Steele in *Singin' In The Rain* (1983), *La Cage Aux Folles* (1986) and *Joseph And The Amazing Technicolor Dreamcoat* (1991).

London Palladium

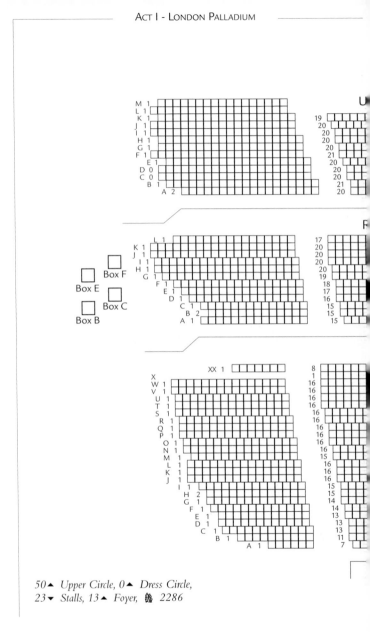

50▲ Upper Circle, 0▲ Dress Circle,
23▼ Stalls, 13▲ Foyer, ♿ 2286

London Palladium

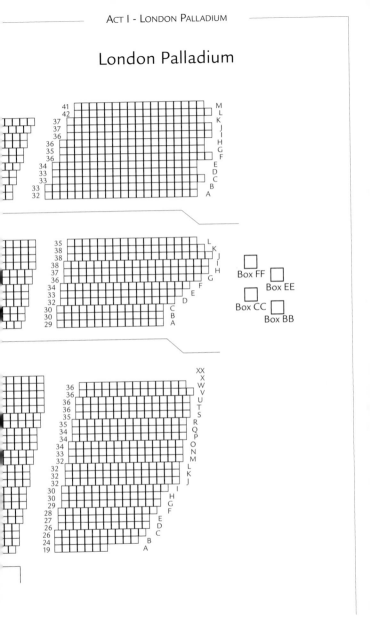

Lyceum

⌨ *Wellington Street, WC2E 7DA*

☎ *0870 243 9000*

✒ *www.apollo-leisure.co.uk*

⊖ *Covent Garden/Holborn/Temple*

🚌 *1, 4, 6, 9, 11, 13, 15, 23, 26, 59, 68, 76, 77A, 91, 168, 171, 172*

🚆 *Charing Cross*

ⓟ *Drury Lane/Shelton Street*

✱ *Air Condition*   ⊲⟩ *Infra-red*

♿ *Stalls*

☆ *Elaborately painted murals in the auditorium*

The Lyceum opened in 1772 as a space for exhibitions, concerts and lectures, as well as hosting circus and other events. When Drury Lane burnt down in 1809 the company transferred, taking their theatre license with them, to the renamed Theatre Royal Lyceum. It became the Theatre Royal English Opera House when they moved back to Drury Lane, once again unable to present plays. The original Lyceum was itself then destroyed by fire and was replaced with a Samuel Beazley designed building which opened in 1834. It presented opera, burletta and other entertainments until the monopoly of Patent theatres was broken in 1843, and eventually became known as the Royal Lyceum Theatre. When the Covent Garden burnt down in 1856, its company moved in until their theatre was rebuilt. Plays began to be presented and in 1871 Henry Irving first appeared here in *The Bells*, a sensation which he followed with *The Pickwick Papers*. Irving took over the theatre in 1878 and appeared in melodramas and lavish Shakespeare productions, with Ellen Terry as his leading lady, until a final performance as Shylock in 1902. The building was in a poor condition and was demolished, except for the façade and portico, and replaced by the current theatre, which was designed as a music hall by Bertie Crew in 1904. The interior, in a lavish baroque style with painted panels was likened to a brothel. Unable to stand the competition from the Coliseum, it was acquired by the Melville brothers in 1909, who switched to a formula of melodrama, mostly written by themselves, combined with annual pantomimes. This later broadened out into opera and ballet again. It was sold for development in 1938 and finally closed with John Gielgud as Hamlet in 1939 uttering a curtain speech cry of "Long live the Lyceum!". For thirty years from 1945 it was used as a dance hall before finally closing again. A season of the National Theatre's promenade production of *The Mysteries* (1982) reawakened interest, and after many near misses it was restored and reopened with *Jesus Christ Superstar* in 1996. Since 1999 The Lyceum has been the venue for The Disney corporation's lavish adaptation of *The Lion King*.

The Lion King

81

Lyceum

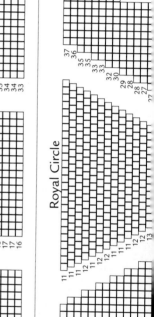

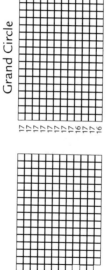

Grand Circle

Royal Circle

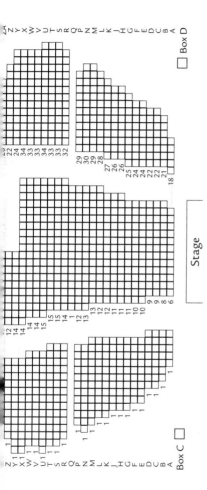

Stage

Box C

Box D

85 ◄ *Upper Circle, 32 ◄ Dress Circle*
7 ▼ *Stalls, 3 ◄ Foyer,* 🏛 *1,899*

Lyric

⌨ *Shaftesbury Avenue, W1V 7DH*
☎ *020 7494 5045*
✍ *www.rutheatres.com*
⊖ *Piccadilly Circus*
🚌 *14, 19, 38*
🚃 *Charing Cross*
ℙ *Brewer Street/Denman Street*
✈ *Air Condition*　◁ *Infra-red*
♿ *Dress Circle*
☆ *Only remaining London theatre with an entrance canopy covering the full width of the pavement*

This is the oldest surviving theatre on the new street called Shaftesbury Avenue that was laid down in 1886. It was designed by C J Phipps on the site of a former anatomical theatre and museum, the Windmill Street façade of which remains, and opened in 1888. The exterior, which is domestic in scale, is of Franco-Flemish Renaissance style in red brick and Portland stone. The auditorium, a U rather than the conventional horseshoe shape, has Corinthian columns supporting the boxes and attractive plasterwork in the large panel above the proscenium. The foyer and bars were extensively reworked in contemporary style by Michel Rosenauer in 1932. Refurbishment and restoration in 1992 comfortably reconciled the two styles. Although conceived as a home for operetta, opening with a transfer of a comic opera *Dorothy*, apart from two W S Gilbert operas *The Mountebanks* (1892) and *His Excellency* (1894), it has mostly seen plays or musicals. The Italian actress Eleonora Duse made her London debut here in *La Dame Aux Camelias*, *Fedora* and *A Doll's House* in 1893. She never wore make up and could blush or pale at will. Wilson Barrett wrote and starred in a religious drama *At The Sign Of The Cross* (1896), a sensation which brought people into the theatre who had never been before. Barrett followed this with *Daughters of Babylon* (1897), although in private admitted he was a believer only as far as the box office was concerned. Oscar Strauss's *The Chocolate Soldier* (1910) based on *Arms And The Man*, the first of George Bernard Shaw's plays to be turned into a musical, received its London production here. Among the premieres staged here were *Lilac Time* (1922), J B Priestley's *Dangerous Corner* (1932), Alan Ayckbourn's *How The Other Half Loves* (1972), Alan Bennett's *Habeas Corpus* (1973) with Alec Guinness – in a unique piece of recasting Bennett took over the role of Mrs Swabb when Patricia Hayes left – and, 200 years after it was written, Fanny Burney's *A Busy Day* (2000). During the run of Joe Orton's black comedy *Loot* (1984), in which a dead body is constantly being hidden from a detective, Leonard Rossiter (playing the detective) died of a heart attack in his dressing room during a performance.

Lyric

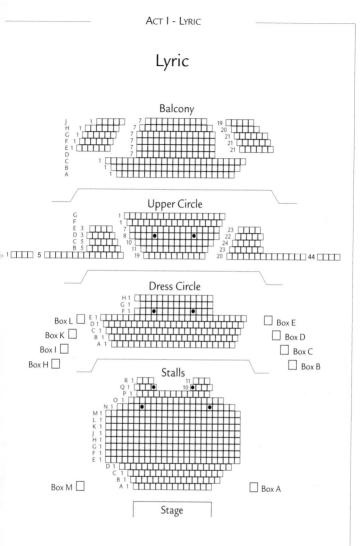

45▲ Balcony, 25▲ Upper Circle, 0▲ Dress Circle, 25▼ Stalls
4▲ Foyer, 🐌 949

Royal National Theatre

⌨ *Upper Ground, South Bank, SE1 9PX*

☎ *020 7452 3000*

✐ *www.nt-online.org*

⊖ *Waterloo*

🚌 *1, 4, 26, 59, 68, 76, 77, 168, 171, 172, 176, 188, 211, 243, 341*

🚃 *Waterloo*

Ⓟ *Beneath the theatre*

✈ *Air Condition*   ◀ *Infra-red*

☆ *Restaurant, bookshop, exhibition and bars open all day, and pre show entertainment. Cottesloe must be accessed from a separate entrance on the eastern side of the building*

Cottesloe

♿ *Dress Circle*

22 ▲ Upper Circle

0 ▲ Dress Circle

10 ▼ Stalls

0 ▲ Foyer

🎭 *Up to 400 depending on configuration*

Royal National Theatre

Although a National Theatre had first been suggested in 1848, serious consideration was sparked by a report by Harley Granville-Barker and William Archer in 1904, and the first site in Gower Street was acquired in 1913. George Bernard Shaw 'turned the first sod' on a site in South Kensington in 1938, and Queen Elizabeth the Queen Mother laid a foundation stone next to the Royal Festival Hall in 1951. An actual company was set up in 1962 under Laurence Olivier, but the building, at a fourth location, did not open until 1976. Although the planning and construction period was shorter than at the Barbican, the National suffered from a similar change in public taste and theatrical practice. Designed by Denys Lasden, the uncompromisingly unadorned boarded concrete is not universally popular, although it is easier to navigate than the Barbican. It comprises three theatres: the Olivier, an open stage derived from a Greek style arena, the Lyttleton, a wide proscenium theatre, and the Cottesloe, a flexible studio space squeezed in as an afterthought, which has become the most popular of the three venues. The company gave its first performance in 1962 with Peter O'Toole as *Hamlet* in its temporary home at the Old Vic – where it remained for 14 years. The National attracted the best actors of its time and rapidly gained a high reputation presenting a repertoire of British and European classics. Its first world premiere, Peter Shaffer's *Royal Hunt Of The Sun* (1964) was equally successful, as was the first work by an untried author, Tom Stoppard's *Rosencrantz And Guildenstern Are Dead* (1967). Olivier gave his last stage performance in Trevor Griffiths' *The Party* (1973) and was succeeded by Peter Hall. He eventually moved the existing repertoire into the Lyttleton, opening with Albert Finney as *Hamlet*, even though the rest of the building was not finished. Richard Eyre became Director in 1988, and was followed by Trevor Nunn in 1997. Among the landmark productions were Peter Shaffer's *Amadeus* (1979), *Guys And Dolls* (1982), *The Mysteries* (1985), David Hare's and Howard Brenton's *Pravda* (1985), Alan Bennett's *The Madness Of George III* (1991), David Hare's Trilogy: *Racing Demon, Murmuring Judges* and *The Absence Of War* (1993), Patrick Marber's *Closer* (1998), *Carousel* (1998), and *My Fair Lady* (2001). In 1999 Nunn returned the National to its roots with an ensemble of actors playing across the repertoire of productions including *Money, The Merchant Of Venice* and *Summerfolk*. History was made by Alan Ayckbourn's *House* and *Garden* (2000) when two plays were performed simultaneously in the Lyttleton and Olivier with the same cast.

Olivier

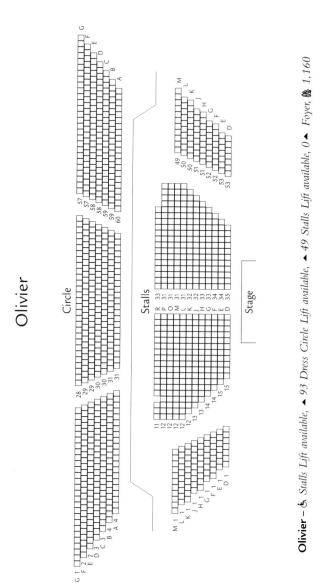

Circle

Stalls

Stage

Olivier – ⛐ *Stalls Lift available,* ▲ *93 Dress Circle Lift available,* ▲ *49 Stalls Lift available,* 0 ◀ *Foyer,* 🏛 *1,160*

Lyttleton

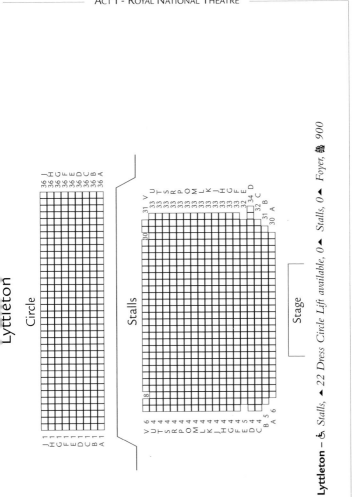

Circle

Stalls

Stage

Lyttleton – ♿ Stalls, ◂ 22 Dress Circle Lift available, 0 ◂ Stalls, 0 ◂ Foyer, 🕮 900

New Ambassadors

⌨ *West Street, WC2H 9ND*

☏ *020 7369 1761*

✎ *www.newambassadors.com*

⊖ *Covent Garden/Leicester Square*

🚌 *14, 19, 24, 29, 38, 176*

🚆 *Charing Cross*

Ⓟ *Shelton Street/Upper St Martin's Lane*

✱ *Air Condition*

☆ *A sculpture next to the box office marks the record-breaking run of*
   The Mousetrap

Conceived as a pair with the St Martin's next door, and designed by twinning expert W G R Sprague, the Ambassadors opened in 1913. The site is very restricted in all directions and the building is a great feat of compression. Legend has it that it was about to open when it was realised that there was no box office, and because the foyer was too small to build one, the ladies toilet had to be converted to fill the bill – although this seems an unlikely oversight for someone like Sprague. It has a simple classical façade in red brick and stucco. The auditorium is a miniature version of Sprague's other theatres, an intimate elegant Louis XVI style, decorated with ambassadorial crests. These were painted out at the outbreak of hostilities in 1914 and only restored in 1958. C B Cochran introduced intimate revue to London here with Alice Delysia in *Odds And Ends* (1914), *More (Odds And Ends)* (1915) and *Pell Mell* (1916). A succession of quality plays introduced new performers to London audiences including Ivor Novello in *Debrau* (1921) Hermione Gingold in *If* (1921), Paul Robeson in *The Emperor Jones* (1925), Margaret Lockwood in *Family Affairs* (1934) and Vivien Leigh in *The Mask Of Virtues* (1935). Revue returned in World War II with *The Gate Revue* (1939), *Swinging At The Gate* (1940), *Sweet And Low* (1943), *Sweeter And Lower* (1944) and *Sweetest And Lowest* (1946) all starring Hermione Gingold. Its place in history was assured when Agatha Christie's *The Mousetrap* (1952) opened, although it transferred to the larger St Martin's (an unheard of step) in 1974. The longest runner since then was the Royal Shakespeare Company production of Christopher Hampton's adaptation of *Les Liaisons Dangerouses* (1986), with Lindsay Duncan and Alan Rickman. The Royal Court moved its Theatre Upstairs productions here while its Sloane Square home was refurbished from 1996 to 1999, dividing the building to create two spaces, using the circle and the stage as separate playing areas. In 1999 it was relaunched as the New Ambassadors, presenting limited runs of new writing or classic revivals by touring companies.

New Ambassadors

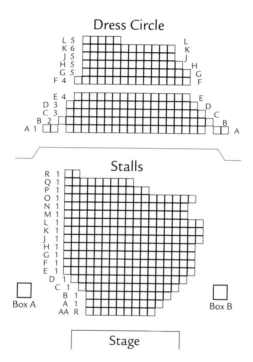

Dress Circle

Stalls

Box A

Box B

Stage

5 ▲ Dress Circle, 26 ▼ 2Stalls, 1 ▲ Foyer, 🐾 418

New London

⌨ *Drury Lane, WC2B 5PW*

☎ *020 7405 0072*

✐ *www.rutheatres.com*

⊖ *Covent Garden/Holborn*

🚌 *1, 8, 19, 25, 38, 55, 59, 68, 91, 98, 168, 171, 188, 242, 243*

🚃 *Charing Cross*

Ⓟ *Beneath the theatre*

✈ *Air Condition* ◁ *Infra-red*

☆ *Art exhibition in the first floor foyer*

Although the present building is one of the few post World War II theatres in London, it occupies a site of taverns and other entertainment establishments dating back to the time of Nell Gwynne, who lived nearby. The Mogul Saloon opened here in 1847 and enjoyed considerable popularity as a music hall, being renamed the Middlesex Music Hall in 1851. It was rebuilt on a grander scale in 1891 before Oswald Stoll took it over and rebuilt it in 1911 as the New Middlesex Theatre of Varieties. This was a grand design by Frank Matcham, possessing the largest frontage of any theatre in London, with an Arabesque style interior. It continued throughout World War I, and was the last music hall in London to retain a Chairman. A new management in 1919 redecorated it in French style, renamed it the Winter Garden and opened it as a theatre. A succession of musical comedies by combinations of P G Wodehouse, Guy Bolton and George Gershwin, *Kissing Time* (1919), *Sally* (1921), *The Cabaret Girl* (1922), *The Beauty Prize* and *Tell Me More* established it as a success in its new role. However after Sophie Tucker in Vivian Ellis's *Follow A Star* (1930) and Gracie Fields in *Walk This Way* (1932) it went into decline, often dark for long periods. Alastair Sim appeared here as Captain Hook in *Peter Pan* (1942) for the first time, a role he continued to play for 26 years. It closed in 1959 and was sold for redevelopment, but although it was demolished in 1965, planning wrangles ensured that construction did not start until the 1970s. The New London theatre opened in 1973 with no real street frontage, as part of a scheme that included a restaurant, offices, shops and flats. Paul Turtkovic, in association with stage designer Sean Kenny, designed it to be flexible, able to be configured in both proscenium arch and theatre in the round formats, with almost one third of the floor area built on a revolve. Enabling it to accommodate any kind of production was supposed to be more attractive to producers, but despite a variety of productions, including Richard Gere in *Grease* (1973), it proved no more successful than before, and became a television studio in 1977. Then came a show that could take advantage of the theatre's flexibility – *Cats* (1981-May 2002), making it London's longest running musical.

New London

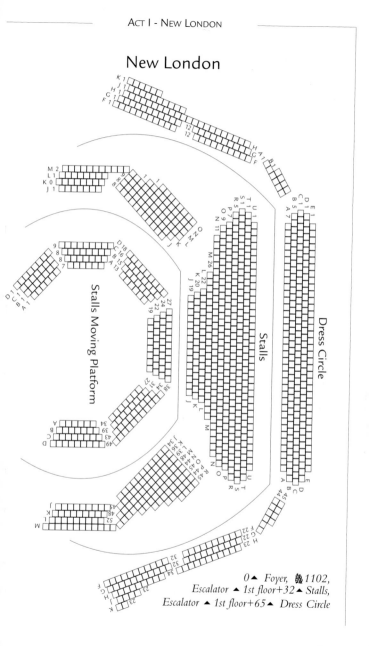

0 ▲ Foyer, 🚻 1102,
Escalator ▲ 1st floor+32 ▲ Stalls,
Escalator ▲ 1st floor+65 ▲ Dress Circle

93

The Old Vic

⌕ *Waterloo Road, SE1 8NB*

☎ *020 7369 1722*

✍ *www.oldvictheatre.com*

⊖ *Waterloo*

🚌 *1, 4, 26, 59, 68, 76, 168, 171, 172, 176, 188, 243, 341*

🚃 *Waterloo*

Ⓟ *On street*

✷ *Air Condition*

♿ *Stalls*

☆ *The auditorium retains the original ceiling, and the unusual barley sugar twist proscenium arch is surmounted by a coat of arms*

The Royal Coburg Theatre was designed by Rudolph Cabanel and opened in 1818. Unlicensed, it became a home for lurid melodramas, although Edmund Kean did appear there in 1831. A new management relaunched it as the Royal Victoria in 1833, but it sank even further to the level of a Blood Tub, staging crude melodrama at very cheap prices. In 1858 sixteen people died and many were injured in a stampede, caused by a false alarm about a fire in the 'fourpenny gallery'. The building was partially reconstructed before opening as the New Victoria Palace music hall in 1871, again unsuccessfully. Emma Cons, a social reformer took it over, and with the interior refurbished by J T Robinson, it reopened in 1881 as the Royal Victoria Hall and Coffee Tavern – "a cheap and decent place of amusement on strict temperance lines". It presented a programme of concerts, opera and scenes from Shakespeare. In 1912 the management passed to Cons' niece Lilian Baylis who had been acting manager since 1898. Despite having no previous experience, Baylis succeeded and went on to lay the foundations of many British cultural institutions. She began presenting full Shakespeare plays at popular prices, the Old Vic becoming in 1923 the first theatre in the world to have completed the entire canon, with actor such as Peggy Ashcroft, Edith Evans, John Gielgud, Charles Laughton, Laurence Olivier, Ralph Richardson and Sybil Thorndyke. Seasons of opera and ballet were also introduced, and Baylis took over and rebuilt Sadler's Wells theatre in 1931 to accommodate the increasing repertoire. Circulating productions between the venues became too costly and inconvenient, especially when scenery blew off a lorry crossing Waterloo Bridge and disappeared into the Thames. Ballet and opera moved permanently to Sadler's Wells in 1935, later developing into the Royal Ballet and English National Opera. Drama continued after Baylis' death in 1937, moving to the West End after bomb damage closed the building. Reopening in 1950, it continued to present plays, including the entire Shakespeare canon again, until 1963 when it was succeeded by the National Theatre Company, which remained until 1976. It then fell on hard times and was often dark, until sold to Ed Mirvish who restored it to the best condition it had ever seen in 1983. Despite attempts to set up new companies by Jonathan Miller and Peter Hall it has failed to find a new role or continuing success.

The Old Vic

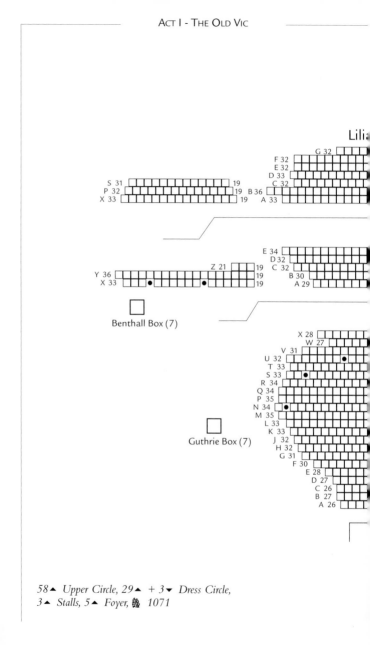

Lili

G 32
F 32
E 32
D 33
C 32
B 36   A 33

S 31   19
P 32   19
X 33   19

E 34
D 32
C 32
B 30
A 29

Z 21   19
Y 36   19
X 33   19

Benthall Box (7)

X 28
W 27
V 31
U 32
T 33
S 33
R 34
Q 34
P 35
N 34
M 35
L 33
K 33
J 32
H 32
G 31
F 30
E 28
D 27
C 26
B 27
A 26

Guthrie Box (7)

58▲ Upper Circle, 29▲ + 3▼ Dress Circle,
3▲ Stalls, 5▲ Foyer, 🏛 1071

The Old Vic

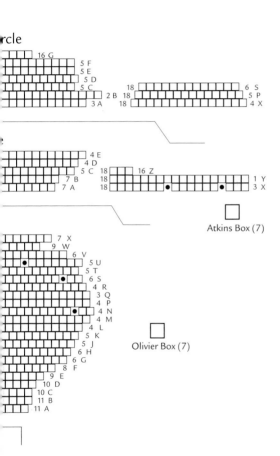

rcle

16 G
5 F
5 E
5 D
5 C
2 B   18   18   18   6 S
3 A   18   5 P
4 X

4 E
4 D
5 C   18   16 Z
7 B   18   1 Y
7 A   18   3 X

Atkins Box (7)

7 X
9 W
6 V
5 U
5 T
6 S
4 R
3 Q
4 P
4 N
4 M
4 L
5 K
5 J
6 H
6 G
8 F
9 E
10 D
10 C
11 B
11 A

Olivier Box (7)

Open Air

- ⌨ *Inner Circle, Regent's Park, NW1 4NP*
- ☎ *020 7486 2431*
- ✍ *www.open-air-theatre.org.uk*
- �{ *Baker Street*
- 🚌 *2, 13, 18, 27, 30, 74, 82, 113, 139, 274, C2*
- 🚆 *Marylebone*
- Ⓟ *On street*
- ✸ *Completely* ◁ *FM Assisted Listening System*
- ♿ *Stalls*
- ☆ *Performances from June to September with extra matinees to cater for school parties*

Open air productions of Shakespeare in Regent's Park were given by Ben Greet and his Woodland Players for a number of years from 1900 onwards. The idea was revived successfully in 1932, with performances of a 'black and white' production of *Twelfth Night* which had been running at the New Theatre. This resulted in a permanent open air theatre being set up in 1933 by Sydney Carrol and Robert Atkins, who continued to run it until 1960. A stage was built in front of existing trees, with shrubs planted at the sides to define it. The audience were seated in deck chairs on the facing slope with park benches at the rear. Lights and speakers were hung in trees. The programmes have mostly been Shakespeare, although Shaw's *The Six Of Calais* (1934) premiered here, and ballet and opera have also been presented. Among the actors who performed here in the early days were Gladys Cooper, Jack Hawkins, Deborah Kerr, Vivien Leigh, Anna Neagle and Jessica Tandy. In 1962 a new stage was built, and David Conville took over, forming the New Shakespeare Company which has been the resident company since. In 1975 the present stadium style building designed by Howell, Killick and Partridge was constructed, providing tip-up seating, with bar and food facilities beneath. This was extended by Haworth Tompkins in 2000 to provide enhanced technical and catering facilities. In recent years the season has developed into a pattern of two Shakespeares and a musical (particularly those with Shakespearean origin such as *The Boys From Syracuse* and *Kiss Me Kate*), plus a children's play presented in the mornings and afternoons. Unsurprisingly the most frequently performed play has been *A Midsummer Night's Dream*, the most regular Bottom being Robert Atkins, followed by the current Artistic Director Ian Talbot (also one of the great Toads in *Toad Of Toad Hall*). Other recent performers include Anthony Andrews, Michael Crawford, Edward Fox, Jeremy Irons, Felicity Kendal and Robert Stephens. Despite the vagaries of British weather, very few performances are actually cancelled each year. The time when stage lights take over as daylight fades is an experience of great theatrical magic not to be missed.

Where's Charley, Open Air

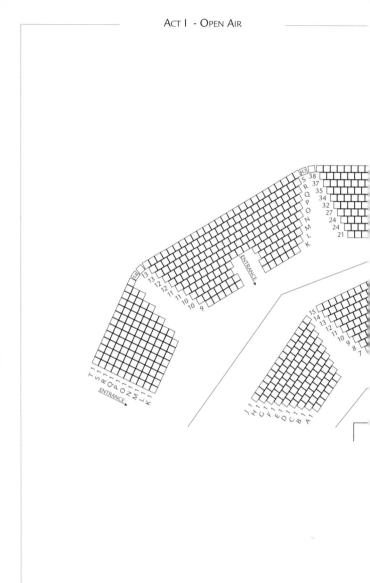

0 ▲ Stalls, 0 ▲ Foyer, 🎭 1,187

Open Air

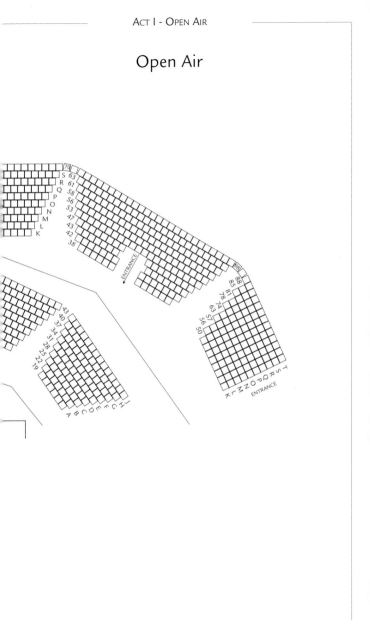

Palace

⌨ *Cambridge Circus, W1V 8AY*
☎ *020 7413 3311*
✎ *www.rutheatres.com*
⊖ *Leicester Square / Tottenham Court Road*
🚌 *14, 19, 24, 29, 38, 176*
🚃 *Charing Cross*
Ⓟ *Cambridge Circus / Wardour Street*
◀ *Infra-red*
♿ *Stalls*

Designed by T E Colcutt and G H Holloway under the supervision of impresario Richard D'Oyly Carte, and occupying a whole block, the Palace opened as the Royal English Opera House in 1891. The red brick and terracotta façade is in Renaissance style, with three bays containing groups of arcaded windows, friezes, statuary and domed octagonal towers to each side of the main frontage and was restored in 1989. Its commanding position makes it a London landmark. Inside the foyer, the grand staircase and Circle Bars are of marble. The long Stalls Bar of gilt, ornate plasterwork and mirrors remains in its original state. The stage was constructed to take the sliding scenery of the period and this also remains largely intact. It was intended to be the home of English opera, and opened with *Ivanhoe* by Arthur Sullivan and Julian Sturgess, but this was a complete flop, after which D'Oyly Carte tried French opera, and then Sarah Bernhardt as Cleopatra, equally unsuccessfully. Disillusioned, he sold out and it became the Palace Theatre of Varieties in 1892. Most of the great music hall artists of the time appeared here, and Pavlova made her London debut in 1910. Its peak as a music hall came with the staging of the first Royal Command Variety Performance in 1912, causing Oswald Stoll to comment "The Cinderella of the arts at last went to the Ball". Public interest moved on to revue and so came *The Passing Show* (1914) with Clara Beck, *Bric-à-Brac* (1915) with Gertie Millar, *Vanity Fair* (1916) and *Airs And Graces* (1917). In the next craze it became a cinema. Live performance returned with the premieres of the musical comedies *No. No. Nanette* (1925), *The Girl Friend* (1927), *The Gay Divorcee* (1933), Cole Porter's *Anything Goes* (1935) and Rodgers and Hart's *On Your Toes* (1937). During World War II Jack Hulbert and Cecily Courtneige starred in a succession of shows including *Under Your Hat* (1938), *Full Swing* (1942) and *Something In The Air* (1943). In the 1950s the Palace was one of the theatres used by Peter Daubeny's World Theatre Seasons and it was also here that John Osbourne's *The Entertainer* (1957) starring Laurence Olivier transferred from the Royal Court. Its recent repertoire has included some of London's longest running shows *The Sound Of Music* (1961), *Jesus Christ Superstar* (1972) and *Les Miserables* (1985).

Palace

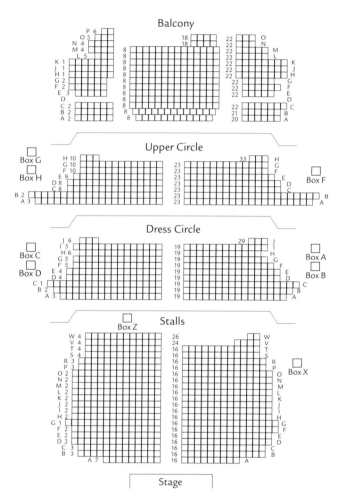

77▲ *Balcony,* 56▲ *Upper Circle,* 30▼ *Dress Circle ,* 22▼ +18▲ *Stalls*
2▲ *Foyer,* ♿*1400*

Peacock

⌧   *Portugal Street, WC2A 2HT*
☎   *020 7863 8222*
⌨   *www.sadlers-wells.com*
⊖   *Covent Garden / Holborn / Temple*
🚌   *1, 4, 6, 9, 11, 13, 76, 77A, 91, 168, 171, 172, 176, 188, 243, 341*
🚃   *Charing Cross*
Ⓟ   *Drury Lane / On street*
♿   *Dress Circle*
☆   *Dickens Old Curiosity Shop is located opposite the rear of the building*

The first theatre on this site, which opened in 1911 and occupied a whole block, was the London Opera House, conceived by American impresario Oscar Hammerstein as a rival to the Covent Garden. It was a grand building designed by Bertie Crewe with a interior of elegance and extravagance. Unfortunately for Hammerstein Covent Garden had the London rights to the most popular works, and the best known singers under contract, and he was forced to close. Seasons of variety, films, plays and pantomimes followed with little success. Oswald Stoll took it over and in 1917 renamed it the Stoll Picture Theatre with a successful formula combining a film with a resident Grand Orchestra featuring singers and instrumentalists. Live entertainment returned in 1941 with twice nightly variety and pantomime. After Stoll died in 1942 it became the Stoll Theatre, and presented revivals of *Lilac Time*, *Show Boat* and *The Student Prince*. In 1947 the stage was converted to an ice rink for a series of Ice Spectacles. The Festival Ballet, later to become English National Ballet, launched here successfully in 1951, and dance and opera seasons, interspersed with occasional musicals and transfers became the norm. The most successful were the Gershwin's *Porgy And Bess* (1952) and *Kismet* (1955). After a season by the Stratford Memorial Theatre of *Titus Andronicus* (1957) with Laurence Olivier and Vivien Leigh it closed and was sold for office development with the proviso that a theatre be included. In 1960 the current building opened as the Royalty Theatre, entirely underground and with the entrance moved to a side street. The interior was of contemporary design, and the stage had an adjustable proscenium arch to accommodate musicals or plays, but after a succession of short runs in 1961 it reverted to films. It returned to live shows with *Oh! Calcutta* (1970) its only real success, before becoming a television studio. When live shows returned in 1986 once again these were mostly short runs of opera and dance. In 1996 the London School of Economics took over the building for educational use, renaming it the Peacock Theatre. It is operated in partnership with Sadler's Wells which was based here while its own theatre was rebuilt, and continues to programme visits by British and international dance companies.

Peacock

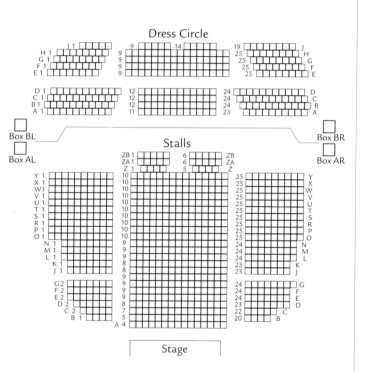

Dress Circle

Stalls

Box BL
Box AL
Box BR
Box AR

Stage

22▼ +7▲ Dress Circle, 44▼ Stalls, 4▲ Foyer, 🏛 1000

Phoenix

⌨ *Charing Cross Road, WC2H 0JP*

☎ *020 7369 1733*

✍ *www.theambassadors.com*

✆ *Leicester Square / Tottenham Court Road*

🚌 *14, 19, 24, 29, 38, 176*

🚃 *Charing Cross*

℗ *Cambridge Circus / Great Russell Street*

♿ *Dress Circle Box*

☆ *Foyer bar contains a display of Noel Coward memorabilia*

In the 1920s this was the site of the Alcazar, a less than high class continuous variety house, whose novelty was three stages, with the audience moving from stage to stage between turns. The current building, which opened in 1930, was designed by the unique combination of Giles Gilbert Scott, Bertie Crewe, and Cecil Masey, with Theodore Komisarjevsky as art director. The exterior is an odd combination of classical stone entrances on two sides of the building, separated by an undistinguished brick block of shops and apartments. The original corner entrance in Charing Cross Road has a loggia with four columns above the canopy topped by an attic with square windows. The current entrance in Phoenix Street is a less formal two storey three bay arcade with twisted columns. Inside is an Art Deco gem of mirrored corridors and bars with painted ceilings. The auditorium has painted panels by Vladimir Polunin after Tintoretto, Titian and Giorgione above the boxes, and the entire safety curtain is a rendition of The Triumph Of Love. Famous actors in well-made plays have provided the Phoenix's staple fare. The opening production was the premiere of Noel Coward's *Private Lives* with Coward, Gertrude Lawrence, Adrianne Allen and Laurence Olivier. This was followed by a succession of flops and a resort to variety, before Coward and Lawrence returned with *Tonight At 8.30* (1936). After this success was again lacking and films were shown in 1938. The first real hit was Cicely Courtneidge in *Under The Counter* (1945). Terrance Ratigan's double bill of *The Browning Version* and *Harlequinade* (1948) fared better than *The Sleeping Prince* (1953) with Laurence Olivier and Vivien Leigh. Other plays to premiere here were Thornton Wilder's *The Skin Of Our Teeth* (1945) with Vivien Leigh, Arthur Miller's *Death Of A Salesman* (1949), John Van Druten's *Bell, Book And Candle* (1954), Tom Stoppard's biggest commercial success *Night And Day* (1978), and Sondheim's *Into The Woods* (1990). In 1976 a Hollywood season saw Rock Hudson and Juliet Prowse in *I Do I Do*, Glynis Johns and Louis Jourdan in *13, Rue De L'Amour*, Lee Remmick in *Bus Stop* and Douglas Fairbanks in *The Pleasure Of His Company*. The unlikely musical *The Canterbury Tales* (1968) proved to be its longest running production.

Phoenix

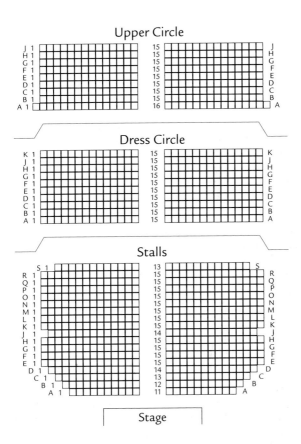

42▲ Upper Circle, 21▲ Dress Circle, 24▼ Stalls, 1▲ Foyer, 🐾 1012

Piccadilly

⌨ *Denman Street, W1V 8DY*

☎ *020 7369 1754*

✍ *www.theambassadors.com*

⊖ *Piccadilly Circus*

🚌 *3, 6, 9, 12, 13, 14, 15, 19, 22, 23, 38, 53, 88, 94, 139, 159*

🚃 *Charing Cross*

Ⓟ *Brewer Street/Denman Street*

✈ *Air Condition*

♿ *Dress Circle*

☆ *A false ceiling was installed which could be lowered to reduce the seating capacity by cutting off the Upper Circle*

Built on the site of former stables, the Piccadilly was designed by Bertie Crewe in conjunction with Edward A Stone, and opened in 1928. The curved exterior of the corner site, looking like stone but actually white cement, echoes the classically influenced Nash buildings in Regent Street. The interior was designed in Art Deco style by French designers Marc-Henri Levy and Gaston Laverdet, but this was replaced by a generic classical scheme in 1955. It has had a troubled history, embracing musicals (many of which flopped) classic drama, and dark periods. After opening with Evelyn Laye in Jerome Kern's *Blue Eyes* it soon succumbed to cinema, showing the first talking picture to be seen in Britain, Al Jolson in *The Singing Fool*. Live shows returned but not very successfully, and in 1937 a new format called *Choose Your Time* was launched, with a continuous programme consisting of newsreel, 'swing-phonic orchestra', individual acts, cartoon and a short comedy play. This fared no better, and transfers of long running shows at reduced prices became the norm until the premiere of Noel Coward's *Blithe Spirit* (1941) – but this soon transferred elsewhere. John Gielgud's *Macbeth* (1942) lived up to the play's unlucky reputation with four of the cast dying and the designer committing suicide; shortly afterwards the building suffered bomb damage and closed. On reopening Noel Coward's revue *Sigh No More* (1945) was followed by *Antony And Cleopatra* (1946), then it was back to transfers. Successes came with the London premieres of Broadway hits, Edward Albee's *Who's Afraid Of Virginia Woolf?* (1964), *Man Of La Mancha* (1968 and 1969) Angela Lansbury in *Gypsy* (1973), Claire Bloom in Tennessee Williams's *A Streetcar Named Desire* (1974) and Henry Fonda as *Clarence Darrow* (1975). In 1980 the Royal Shakespeare Company production of Willy Russell's *Educating Rita* launched the career of Julie Walters. A series of megamusical flops followed with *Mutiny* (1985), *Metropolis* (1989), *King* (1990), and *Which Witch* (1992). It was redeemed by the longest ever West End run of a ballet with Matthew Bourne's *Swan Lake* (1996).

Piccadilly

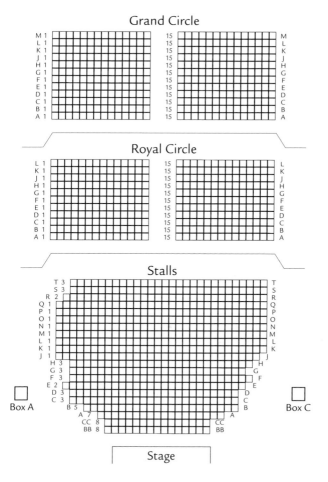

Grand Circle

M 1
L 1
K 1
J 1
H 1
G 1
F 1
E 1
D 1
C 1
B 1
A 1

15 M
15 L
15 K
15 J
15 H
15 G
15 F
15 E
15 D
15 C
15 B
15 A

Royal Circle

L 1
K 1
J 1
H 1
G 1
F 1
E 1
D 1
C 1
B 1
A 1

15 L
15 K
15 J
15 H
15 G
15 F
15 E
15 D
15 C
15 B
15 A

Stalls

T 3
S 3
R 2
Q 1
P 1
O 1
N 1
M 1
L 1
K 1
J 1
H 3
G 3
F 3
E 2
D 3
C 3
B 5
A 7
CC 8
BB 8

T
S
R
Q
P
O
N
M
L
K
J
H
G
F
E
D
C
B
A
CC
BB

Box A

Box C

Stage

70▲ Upper Circle, 6▲ Dress Circle, 15▼ Stalls, 1▲ Foyer, 🎭 1,213

109

Playhouse

⌨ *Northumberland Avenue, WC2N 5DE*

☎ *020 7316 4747*

⊖ *Charing Cross/Embankment*

🚌 *3, 6, 9, 11, 12, 13, 15, 23, 24, 29, 30, 53, 77A, 88, 91, 139, 159,*

🚃 *Charing Cross*

Ⓟ *Trafalgar Square/Limited on street*

✷ *Air Condition*   ◁ *Induction Loop*

♿ *Stalls*

☆ *The safety curtain is painted in the style of the original act drop*

Rumour has it that the first theatre on this site, the Royal Avenue (1882), was built because its owner Sefton Parry believed that the South Eastern Railway Company would want to acquire it for an extension to Charing Cross Station, at great profit to himself. He was wrong. It opened with a French comic opera *Madame Favart*, which was followed by more of the same, but a change of policy brought drama with the first plays of George Bernard Shaw, *Arms And The Man* (1894), and Somerset Maugham, *A Man Of Honour* (1901). The reconstruction of the theatre to a second design by the original architect F H Fowler was almost completed in 1905, when part of the station collapsed onto the site, killing six people, injuring twenty six, and badly damaging the theatre. When compensation of £20,000 was finally received the current theatre was constructed. A new design by Detmar Blow and Fernand Billerey, retaining most of the exterior but with a new interior, opened in 1907 as the Playhouse. The façade is of Portland stone in French Renaissance style. The auditorium in Franco-Venetian style has fine plasterwork, upper boxes supported by statuary and with ornamental lamp post light fittings, and balustraded circle fronts. Gladys Cooper, one of the few female actor managers, starred with Gerald du Maurier in many of the plays she produced here, which included *White Cargo* (1924) and *The Painted Veil* (1931), and the premiere of Maugham's *Home And Beauty* (1919). Apart from seasons by Nancy Price's People's National Theatre (1938-39) and the Old Vic, when Peter Ustinov's early play *Blow Your Own Trumpet* was shown, it was mostly short runs – one revue lasted only two nights – and dark periods. In 1951 the BBC took it over and many radio comedy programmes, such as *Hancock's Half Hour* and *The Goon Show*, and panel games were recorded here over the next twenty five years. Music programmes, some of which featured early appearances by The Beatles and The Rolling Stones were also produced here. Abandoned for ten years, the Playhouse was restored and reopened in 1987, but a succession of managements, including a Peter Hall Company season of Tennessee Williams's *The Rose Tattoo*, *Twelfth Night* and Molière's *Tartuffe* and *A Doll's House* (1996) have failed to break the short run/dark spell cycle.

Playhouse

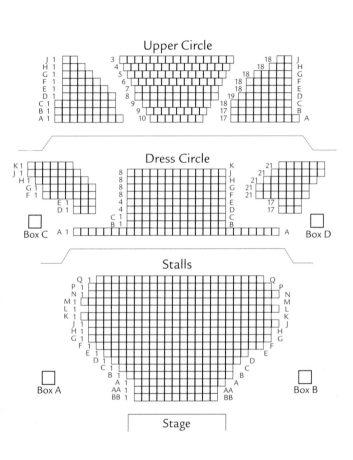

Upper Circle

Dress Circle

Box C

Box D

Stalls

Box A

Box B

Stage

88▲ Upper Circle, 29▲ Dress Circle, 0▲ Stalls, 3▲ Foyer, 🐾 *756*

Prince Edward

- 🎬 *Old Compton Street, W1V 6HS*
- ☎ *020 7447 5400*
- ⊖ *Leicester Square / Tottenham Court Road*
- 🚌 *14, 19, 24, 29, 38, 176*
- 🚆 *Charing Cross*
- ℗ *Cambridge Circus / Wardour Street*
- ✈ *Air Condition* ◁ *Infra-red*
- ♿ *Dress Circle / Royal Box*
- ☆ *Unusual circular foyer and stepped loges at the sides of the auditorium*

Built on the site of The Emporium, a former royal draper's shop, the Prince Edward was designed by Edward A Stone, with an interior by French designers Marc-Henri Levy and Gaston Laverdet and opened in 1930. The red brick exterior is in the style of an Italian palazzo, incorporating a loggia colonnade at first floor level, whose windows were originally fitted with green shutters. The Art Deco auditorium with rectilinear patterns made use of a new material Marb-L-Cote, and the proscenium was framed in amber Rene Lalique glass – no longer extant. It opened with the show *Rio Rita (1930)*, but despite trying musicals, cabaret with *Josephine Baker* (1933), non-stop revue, talkies and trade shows the theatre was not successful. It was reconstructed by Stone into a cabaret-restaurant with a dance floor, staircases from the stalls to the dress circle and stepped loges at the sides, reopening in 1936 as the London Casino. With lavish shows such as *Follies Parisiennes* it soon became the most profitable entertainment venue in London taking £7000 a week. Having closed during the Blitz in 1940, it re-emerged as the Queensbury All Services Club in 1942 with on-stage seating round a boxing ring, and remained as such until the end of World War II. Theatre returned with *Pick Up Girl* (1946), *The Dancing Years* (1947), variety, ballet seasons and pantomime. In 1949 Robert Nesbitt's *Latin Quarter* cabaret show was staged and ran on into several editions. In 1954 Cinerama arrived in London with a huge semicircular screen installed on the stage. When this fad was over it remained as a cinema showing long runs including *How The West Was Won* (1962) and *2001: A Space Odyssey* (1968). In 1974 a mixed programme of pantomime, live shows and films was launched with *Cinderella* starring Twiggy, but most shows were flops. Its fortunes changed in 1978 when it reverted to the original name of Prince Edward with Tim Rice and Andrew Lloyd Webber's *Evita*. Since then it has seen a succession of long running musicals, *Chess* (1986), *Anything Goes* (1989), *Crazy For You* (1993), and *Mamma Mia!* (2000) interspersed with a few flops and the continually reworked *Martin Guerre* (1996). A refurbishment in 1992 restored the Theatre to something approaching its original design scheme.

Prince Edward

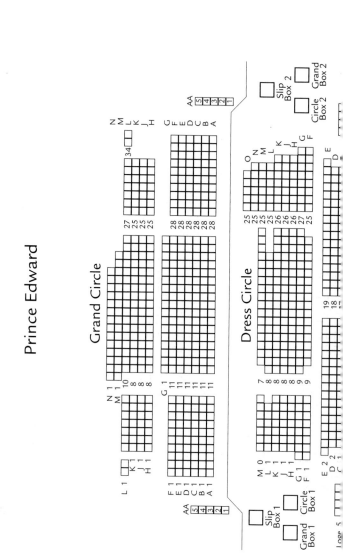

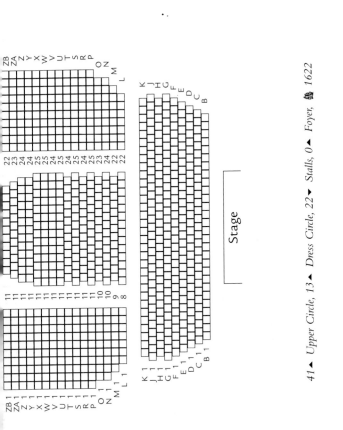

ZB
ZA
Z
Y
X
W
V
U
T
S
R
P
O
N
M
L

22 23 24 24 25 25 24 25 25 24 25 24 23 24 22 22

11 11 11 11 11 11 11 11 11 10 10 9 8

ZB 1
ZA 1
Z 1
Y 1
X 1
W 1
V 1
U 1
T 1
S 1
R 1
P 1
O 1
N 1
M 1
L 1

K
J
H
G
F
E
D
C
B

K 1
J 1
H 1
G 1
F 1
E 1
D 1
C 1
B 1

Stage

41 ◂ Upper Circle, 13 ◂ Dress Circle, 22 ▾ Stalls, 0 ◂ Foyer, 𝆎 1622

115

Prince of Wales

☐ *Coventry Street, W1V 8AS*
☎ *020 7839 5972*
⊖ *Leicester Square/Piccadilly Circus*
🚌 *3, 6, 9, 12, 13, 14, 15, 19, 22, 23, 38, 53, 88, 94, 139, 159*
🚃 *Charing Cross*
Ⓟ *Denman Street/Whitcomb Street*
✈ *Air Condition* ◁ *Infra-red*
♿ *Stalls*
☆ *Stalls Bar has an extensive collection of posters from previous productions*

The first theatre on the site was designed by C J Phipps in Moorish style, and opened in 1884 as the Prince's. It was renamed the Prince Of Wales in 1886 when another theatre of that name closed and became a Salvation Army hostel. The current building, which was designed by Robert Cromie in restrained Art Deco style, opened in 1937. The exterior is in artificial stone with a commanding circular tower above its corner entrance. The wide and shallow auditorium is on just two levels, with the Circle front only 21 feet from the pit rail. Much of the original decoration was removed in 1963 and the interior now has a simple scheme. The large bar beneath the Stalls boasts a dance floor and a 46 foot long bar. It has been notable for introducing a number of theatrical ideas to London. *L'Enfant Prodigue* (1891) 'a wordless play' with mimes led to the establishment of the first British Pierrot troupe. *In Town* (1892) described as a 'musical farce' was a prototype musical comedy, and its success spawned others including *Gaiety Girl* (1893), *Gentleman Joe* (1895), *The School Girl* (1903) and *Lady Madcap* (1904). The famous André Charlot revues *Bran Pie* (1919), *A to Z* (1921), *Charlot's Revue* (1924) and *Charlot's Show* (1926) featured Gertrude Lawrence, Beatrice Lillie, Jessie Matthews and Jack Buchanan. These were followed by less prestigious non-stop revue until the theatre closed in 1937. The new building opened with *Les Folies de Paris et Londres*, and continued with similar shows. *Strike A New Note* (1943) brought comedian Sid Field to the West End, he also starred in *Strike It Again* (1944), *Piccadilly Hayride* (1946), and *Harvey* (1949). Mae West appeared in *Diamond Lil* (1948). The 1950s saw a succession of variety spectaculars with Frankie Howerd, Norman Wisdom, Benny Hill, Max Bygraves and others. It then became home to American shows *The World Of Suzy Wong* (1959), Neil Simon's *Come Blow Your Horn* (1962), Barbra Striesand in *Funny Girl* (1962), *Sweet Charity* (1967), and *Promises Promises* (1969). Recent years have seen a mixture of new and revived musicals including *Underneath The Arches* (1982), *South Pacific* (1988), *Aspects Of Love* (1989), *Annie Get Your Gun* (1992), and *City Of Angels* (1993).

Prince Of Wales

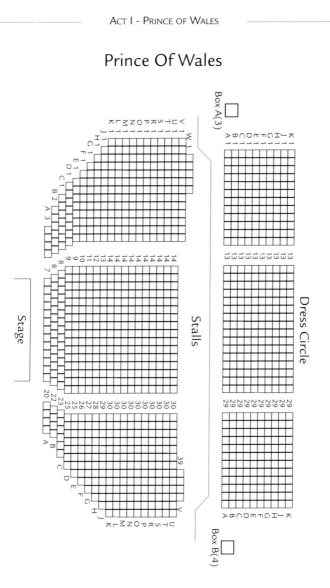

21▲ +3▼ Dress Circle, 4▼ Stalls, 0▲ Foyer, 🐾 1133

Queen's

- ⌨ *Shaftesbury Avenue, W1V 8BA*
- ☎ *020 7494 5065*
- ✐ *www.rutheatres.com*
- ⊖ *Piccadilly Circus*
- 🚌 *14, 19, 38*
- 🚃 *Charing Cross*
- Ⓟ *Brewer Street/Wardour Street*
- ✈ *Air Condition* ◁ *Infra-red*
- ♿ *Dress Circle*
- ☆ *Photographs of the original Sprague façade and foyer can be found in the lobby*

This W G R Sprague designed theatre opened in 1907 and, like his Strand and Aldwych theatres, it bookends a whole block with the Gielgud Theatre. The two theatres were originally very similar, with Queen's being the slightly larger and more imposing of the two. It suffered severe bomb damage in 1942 and remained closed until 1959. A dull contemporary exterior and front of house was designed by Bryan Westwood and Hugh Casson, while the auditorium was restored to something approaching its original form. This is in similar grand Louis XVI style to the Gielgud, in red, white and gold, but even more splendid, including a domed ceiling with elaborate plasterwork ornamentation in the form of full-length relief figures of muses. The opening show was a flop and various managements tried their hand, including H B Irving producing and starring in some of his father Henry's successes, *The Bells, Louis XI* and *Hamlet* (1909-11). In 1913 'Tango Teas' were introduced, with the stalls transformed into a dance floor with tables surrounding it. The first success was two American comedians in *Potash And Perlmutter* (1914) and its sequel *Potash And Perlmutter In Society* (1916). The 1930s saw a succession of quality productions with Cedric Hardwicke and Edith Evans in Shaw's *The Apple Cart* (1929), the Old Vic production of John Gielgud's *Hamlet* with Donald Wolfit and Martita Hunt, *The Barratts Of Wimpole Street, The Farmer's Wife,* Shaw's *Heartbreak House,* and Robert Morley's first play *Short Story* (1935). There was a Gielgud season (1937) in which he not only starred in *Richard II, The Merchant Of Venice, The Three Sisters* and *The School For Scandal,* but also directed the first two. It reopened in 1959 with Gielgud's Shakespeare recital *The Ages Of Man.* Noel Coward made his final West End appearance here in 1966. Shows which premiered here since include Anthony Newley's *Stop The World I Want To Get Off* (1961), Neil Simon's *The Odd Couple* (1966), Joe Orton's *What The Butler Saw* (1969), Simon Gray's *Otherwise Engaged* (1975), Tom Courtenay in *The Dresser* (1980), Julian Mitchell's *Another Country* (1982), *Shadowlands* (1989) and Stephen Sondheim's *Passion* (1996).

Queen's

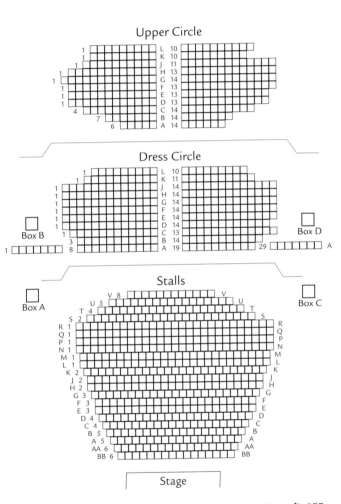

Upper Circle

Dress Circle

Box B

Box D

Stalls

Box A

Box C

Stage

39▲ Upper Circle, 18▲ Dress Circle, 21▼ Stalls, 1▲ Foyer, ♿ *977*

119

Royal Court

⌨ *Sloane Square, SW1W 8AS*
☎ *020 7565 5000*
✎ *www.royalcourttheatre.com*
⊖ *Sloane Square*
🚌 *11, 19, 22, 137, 211, 319, C1*
🚈 *Victoria*
Ⓟ *Semley Place / Warwick Way*
✈ *Air Condition*
⤴ *Infra-red & Induction Loop*
♿ *Stalls & Dress Circle*
☆ *Restaurant, bookshop, and bar open all day*

Jerwood Theatre Upstairs

♿ *Stalls Lift available*
▲ *64 Stalls Lift available*
🦯 *77*

Sloane Square had a theatre on its south side from 1870, when a disused chapel was converted into the New Chelsea, which then became the Belgravia. This was reconstructed as the Royal Court in 1871, and staged the premieres of Arthur Wing Pinero's farces *The Magistrate* (1885), *The Schoolmistress* (1886) and *Dandy Dick* (1887). When redevelopment required its demolition, the present building, designed by Walter Emden and Bertie Crewe, was constructed as a replacement on the east side of the Square, opening in 1888. The exterior is of stone and red brick in Italian Renaissance style and the interior has undergone several reconstructions from its original form of three circles decorated in Empire style. After bomb damage it was remodelled by Robert Cromie in 1952, when the Gallery was shut off and converted into offices, and the rehearsal room at the top of the building was turned into a restaurant. This became the Theatre Upstairs studio theatre in 1971. The building underwent major refurbishment in 2000 by Harworth Tompkins, whose decorative style was to remove the plasterwork and not replace it. The Royal Court enjoyed its first great age under Harley Granville-Barker and J E Vedrenne (1904-07), when 32 plays by 17 authors were presented. Of these 11 were by Shaw including *Man And Superman*, *Major Barbara* and *The Doctor's Dilemma*, plus Galsworthy's *The Silver Box*, and Elizabeth *Votes For Women*. Shaw returned with *Heartbreak House* (1921) and *Back To Methusalah* (1924). The theatre's second golden age dawned in 1956 when the English Stage Company under George Devine took over, dedicated to producing new writing. It was immediately successful, changing the course of British drama with

John Osborne's *Look Back In Anger* (1956), *The Entertainer* (1957) with Laurence Olivier, and *A Patriot For Me* (1965), and Arnold Wesker's *Chicken Soup With Barley* (1958), *Roots* (1959), *I'm Talking About Jerusalem* (1960), *The Kitchen* (1961) and *Chips With Everything* (1962). Other writers included John Arden, Anne Jellicoe, Edward Bond, David Storey, Christopher Hampton, David Hare and Caryl Churchill. It has also presented contemporary European writers, including Beckett, Brecht, Genet, Ionesco and Sartre, and continues to be the 'national theatre of new writing'. Recent discoveries have been Terry Johnson *Hysteria* (1993), Kevin Elyot *My Night With Reg* (1994), Jez Butterworth *Mojo* (1995), Sarah Kane *Blasted* (1996), Mark Ravenhill *Shopping And Fucking* (1996), Martin McDonagh *The Leenane Trilogy* (1997), and Conor McPherson *The Weir* (1997).

Jerwood Theatre Downstairs

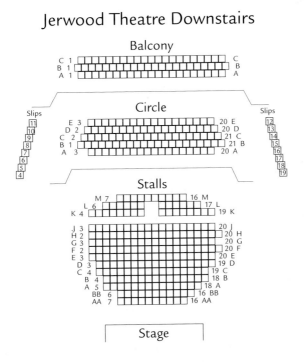

64▲ Upper Circle Lift available, 18▲ Dress Circle Lift available, 20▼ Stalls Lift available, 3▲ Foyer, ♿ 400

121

Royal Opera House

🖳 *Bow Street, Covent Garden, WC2E 9DD*
☎ *020 7304 4000*
🖎 *www.royalopera.org*
⊖ *Covent Garden/Holborn/Temple*
🚌 *1, 4, 6, 9, 11, 13, 15, 23, 26, 59, 68, 76, 77A, 91, 168, 171, 172*
🚃 *Charing Cross*
Ⓟ *Drury Lane/Shelton Street*
✹ *Air Condition* ⤙ *Infra-red*
♿ *Stalls*
☆ *Floral Hall foyer bar, restaurant and bookshop open all day*

Linbury Studio

♿ *Stalls*
27▾ *Dress Circle Lift available*
🐜 *420*

The first theatre on this site was constructed 1732 to house a company holding the second Royal Patent allowing it to perform plays. Among early premieres were Handel's *Alcina* (1735), *Atlanta* (1736) and *Berenice* (1737), the first public performance of a piano (1767), Oliver Goldsmith's *She Stoops To Conquer* (1773), Richard Brinsley Sheridan's *The Rivals* (1775), the pantomime *Aladdin* (1788), and the first melodrama *A Tale Of Mystery* (1802). William Betty, a thirteen year old 'child tragedian' became the rage in 1804 playing major Shakespearean roles including Hamlet. A fire destroyed the building along with Handel's organ and many scores in 1808. When the second theatre opened the following year an attempt was made to raise the prices, provoking the Old Prices Riot, which resulted in the Riot Act being read from the stage and, ultimately, an apology from the management. William Charles Macready revolutionised stage illumination here in 1837 with the introduction of limelight. After considerable interior alterations, the theatre became The Royal Italian Opera in 1847. The current building, designed by Edward M Barry, in Roman Renaissance style with a Corinthian portico incorporating some statuary and bas-reliefs from the previous theatre, opened in 1858. The interior is majestic with a Grand Staircase rising between allegorical paintings to the Crush Bar, a great hall with 20ft high paintings and chandelier. The cream, gold and red auditorium includes a scene of Orpheus playing a lyre above the proscenium. Apart from an earlier conversion from boxes to open seating in the circle levels and a recent re-raking of the stalls to improve sightlines the auditorium remains substantially the same today. It dropped the Italian to become the Royal Opera in 1892 and finally became the

oyal Opera House in 1939. The Covent Garden Opera Company was
tablished in 1946, later becoming the Royal Opera, joined by Sadler's
Jells Ballet, becoming the Royal Ballet in 1956, and they have coex-
ted ever since. An expensive and controversial refurbishment scheme,
at included construction of the Linbury Studio auditorium, almost
rought the ROH to bankruptcy in 1997 but it survived to reopen in
999. The Linbury enables the company to perform small scale and
xperimental work, recitals, and show productions by outside companies.

oyal Opera House

123

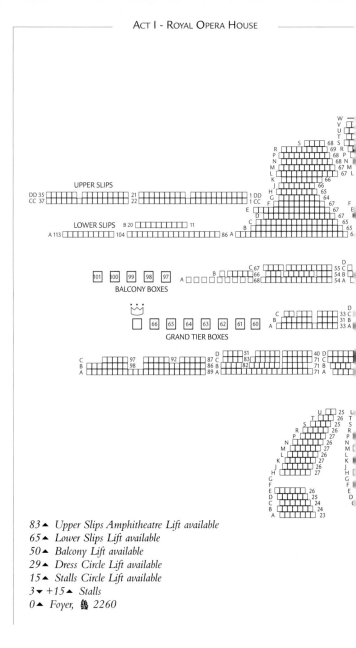

83▲ Upper Slips Amphitheatre Lift available
65▲ Lower Slips Lift available
50▲ Balcony Lift available
29▲ Dress Circle Lift available
15▲ Stalls Circle Lift available
3▼ +15▲ Stalls
0▲ Foyer, ♿ 2260

Royal Opera House

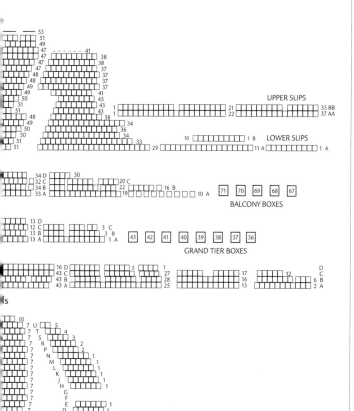

UPPER SLIPS

LOWER SLIPS

BALCONY BOXES

GRAND TIER BOXES

Sadler's Wells

⌨ *Rosebery Avenue, EC1R 4TN*

☎ *020 7863 8000*

✎ *www.sadlerswells.com*

☻ *Angel*

🚌 *19, 38, 341, SWX to Holborn, Aldwych & Waterloo 10 minutes after performance ends*

🚆 *King's Cross*

Ⓟ *On street*

✹ *Air Condition* ⌁ *Infra-red*

♿ *Stalls & 1st Circle*

☆ *Original well in corridor at rear of Stalls, art exhibition in Dress Circle foyer*

Lilian Baylis Studio

♿ *Stalls*

0▲ *Stalls*

0▲ *Foyer*

🎭 *Depends on configuration*

As a place of entertainment this site dates back to 1683 when workmen in the grounds of Thomas Sadler discovered a well, thought to have belonged to an ancient Priory and believed to have possessed miraculous powers. Within the year a pleasure garden with a wooden building known as Sadler's Musick House had been opened, which eventually became Sadler's Wells. In 1753 a resident company of singers, dancers and acrobats was set up and in 1765 the first stone building was opened. By 1780s Grimaldi, Edmund Kean and a troupe of performing dogs were among the attractions. In the 1820s melodramas 'in the aquatic tradition' were performed employing water effects including a tank in which naval battles were re-enacted. Following the breaking of the monopoly of Patent theatres Samuel Phelps took over in 1844 and relaunched it as the Theatre Royal Sadler's Wells. Established as a home for Shakespeare, it presented thirty four of his plays in the next twenty years. After this it was used variously for ice skating, prize fighting, a wash house, a pickle factory, music hall and cinema before final closure in 1906. Lilian Baylis decided it could become a north London equivalent to the Old Vic and raised funds for a new building, designed by F G M Chancellor which opened in 1931. However moving productions back and forth between the two venues became too difficult and costly, and from 1935 the opera and ballet companies took up residence here. It closed following bomb damage in 1940 but reopened with the premiere of Benjamin Britten's *Peter Grimes* (1945). The ballet company moved to Covent Garden in 1946, and the opera company moved to the Coliseum in 1968. Sadler's Wells then became a venue for British touring and foreign opera and dance companies. In 1999 a new theatre designed by RHWL opened, the first in London to be substantially funded by the National Lottery. The post-modern exterior of sharply angled brick and glass is a radical departure from conventional theatre architecture. The feeling of modernity continues inside, with white walls and blonde wood floors in the foyers, and perforated metal used in the auditorium. Thomas Sadler's well has been reopened so patrons can once again take the waters. Regular British visitors have included Northern Ballet Theatre, Rambert Dance Company and Scottish Ballet, and international companies have included Alvin Ailey, Merce Cunningham, Nederlands Dance Theatre, and Paco Pena.

Sadler's Wells

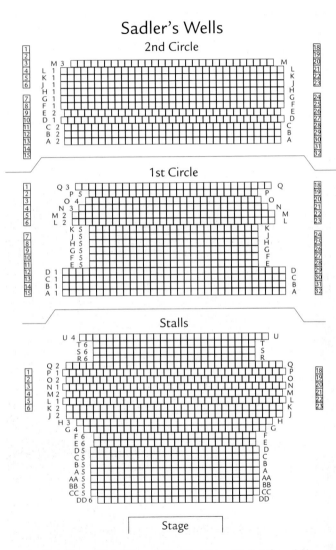

Sadler's Wells

*63▲ Upper Circle Lift available, 42▲ Dress Circle Lift available,
4▲ Stalls, 0▲ Foyer, ♿ 1550*

St Martin's

⌨ *West Street, WC2H 9NH*

☎ *020 7836 1443*

⊖ *Covent Garden / Leicester Square*

🚌 *14, 19, 24, 29, 38, 176*

🚃 *Charing Cross*

Ⓟ *Shelton Street / Upper St Martin's Lane*

✱ *Air Condition*   ◁ *Infra-red & Induction Loop*

☆ *Unique wood panelled auditorium with balustraded circle fronts*

Originally conceived as a pair with the New Ambassadors next door, and designed by twinning expert W G R Sprague, St Martin's opened in 1916, its construction having been delayed by World War I. It has a distinctly grander, larger and later feel than the New Ambassadors, the ashlar-faced exterior boasting a higher roof line supported by four Ionic columns from first floor level. The auditorium eschews plasterwork for English Georgian style walnut panelling, Doric columns, wooden balustraded circle and box fronts, and a glass domed ceiling which was refurbished in 1996. In its early years St Martin's staged important premieres of plays debating contemporary issues including Eugene Brieux's *Damaged Goods* (1917) about sexually transmitted disease, John Galsworthy's *The Skin Game* (1920), Clemence Dane's *A Bill Of Divorcement* (1921) dealing with divorce on the grounds of insanity, and Karel Capek's *RUR – Rossum's Universal Robots* (1923) about the mechanisation of modern life which coined the word 'robot'. Charles McKevoy's story of East End slum life, *The Likes Of Her* (1923) launched the career of Hermione Baddeley here, while Frederick Lonsdale's *Spring Cleaning* (1925) caused a sensation because it included a prostitute among its characters. Also staged here were Reginald Berkley's *The White Chateaux* (1927) questioning the First World War, Rodney Ackland's *Strange Orchestra* (1932) the first modern play directed by John Gielgud, and   s *The Green Bay Tree* (1933) the first play to discuss homosexuality – although it never mentioned the word. During the first production of J B Priestley's *When We Are Married* (1938) Priestley took over the role of the photographer when the actor playing him was injured. After World War II successes were few, and mostly transfers from other theatres. It has run the gamut of thrillers with the premieres from Arnold Ridley's *The Ghost Train* (1925) through Edward Percy's *The Shop At Sly Corner* (1945) and *Guilty Party* (1961) to the modern classic *Sleuth* (1970) with Anthony Quale and Keith Baxter – its longest run to that time. *The Mousetrap* crossed Tower Court from the New Ambassadors in 1974 and has been in residence here ever since. In 1999 the original set (being older than some of its audience) was replaced and was auctioned off to the highest bidder – but nobody seems to know who-wunnit. The cast now changes annually.

St Martin's

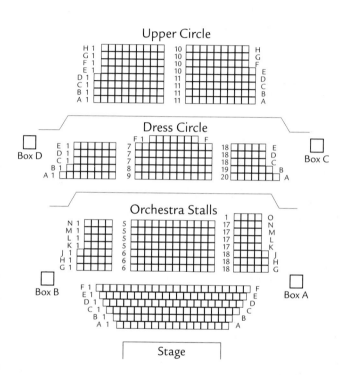

Upper Circle

H 1
G 1
F 1
E 1
D 1
C 1
B 1
A 1

10
10
10
10
11
11
11
11

H
G
F
E
D
C
B
A

Dress Circle

Box D

E 1
D 1
C 1
B 1
A 1

F 1
7
7
7
8
9

F
18
18
18
19
20
A

E
D
C
B

Box C

Orchestra Stalls

N 1
M 1
L 1
K 1
J 1
H 1
G 1

5
5
5
5
6
6
6

1
17
17
17
18
18
18

O
N
M
L
K
J
H
G

Box B

F 1
E 1
D 1
C 1
B 1
A 1

F
E
D
C
B
A

Box A

Stage

28▲ Upper Circle, 3▲ Dress Circle, 29▼ Stalls, 3▲ Foyer, 🐾 550

131

Savoy

- 🖂 *The Strand, WC2R 0ET*
- ☎ *020 7836 8888*
- ⊖ *Charing Cross / Covent Garden*
- 🚌 *6, 9, 11, 13, 15, 23, 77A, 91, 176*
- 🚆 *Charing Cross*
- Ⓟ *Bedfordbury / Trafalgar Square*
- ✈ *Air Condition* ⨾ *Infra-red*
- ♿ *Dress Circle Box*
- ☆ *Fluted auditorium walls covered in aluminium leaf*

The first Savoy theatre was built by impresario Richard D'Oyly Carte on the Embankment, within the precincts of the ancient Savoy Palace, to stage Gilbert and Sullivan operettas. Designed by C J Phipps, it opened in 1881, and was the first public building in the world to be lit entirely by electricity. In 1903 when the Savoy Hotel was built, the theatre's entrance was moved to adjoin the hotel's entrance in Savoy Court. In 1929 it was completely gutted and a new theatre designed by Frank A Tugwell, with interior decoration by Basil Ionides, was constructed. The entrance went back to the Embankment, but after a redesign in a style to match the refurbished Hotel it returned to Savoy Court. Because of its unique position, the exterior has largely been subsumed by the Hotel, although the original Phipps façade can be seen on the Embankment. The interior is a fine example of Art Deco style with indirect lighting via fixtures in plaster cornices, and seating upholstered in an attractive five colour scheme. There is careful detailing on doors and walls, a glass screen in the Dress Circle bar, a group of Egyptian maidens around a large vase, and painted decoration on the walls of the bars and corridors. A fire destroyed the auditorium in 1990 but it was restored to its 1929 splendour in 1993. The theatre first opened with a transfer of *Patience*, and Gilbert and Sullivan operettas which premiered here were *Iolanthe* (1882), *Princess Ida* (1884), *Trial By Jury* (1884), *The Mikado* (1885), *Ruddigore* (1887), *The Yeomen Of The Guard* (1888), *The Gondoliers* (1889), *Utopia Ltd* (1893) and *The Grand Duke* (1896). Revivals have been seen here many times. Another important era was when Harley Granville-Barker and J E Vedrenne transferred their partnership here from the Royal Court in 1907. They produced among others Shaw's *The Devil's Disciple* and *Caesar And Cleopatra* as well as Shakespeare productions from 1912 to 1914. The Savoy production of *Young Woodley* (1928), which transferred from the Arts, launched the career of John Van Druten and the following year saw R C Sherrif's career get underway with *Journey's End*. Robert Morley named his son (the critic Sheridan Morley) after Sheridan Whiteside, the character he played in Kaufman and Hart's *The Man Who Came To Dinner* (1941). Two Noel Coward musical adaptations premiered here, *Sail Away* (1962) and *High Spirits* (1964). In more recent years it has specialised in comedies including William Douglas Home's *The Secretary Bird* (1968) and *Lloyd George Knew My Father* (1972), and Robert Morley returning in *A Ghost On Tiptoe* (1974) and Ben Travers *Banana Ridge* (1976), Michael Frayn's *Noises Off* (1982), and *Plunder* (1996). D'Oyly Carte returned with *HMS Pinafore* (2000), *The Mikado* (2000) and *The Pirates Of Penzance* (2001).

Savoy

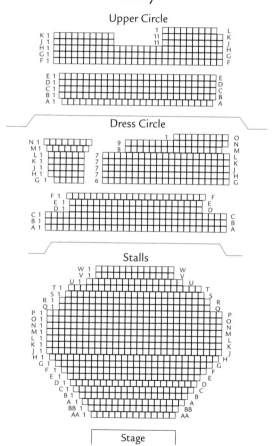

Upper Circle

Dress Circle

Stalls

Stage

2▼ +2▲ *Upper Circle, 30*▼ *Dress Circle, 63*▼ *Stalls, 0*▲ *Foyer,* 🎭 *1158*

Shaftesbury

⌨ *Shaftesbury Avenue, WC2H 8DP*

☏ *020 7379 5399*

⊖ *Covent Garden/Holborn/Tottenham Court Road*

🚌 *8, 10, 14, 19, 24, 25, 29, 38, 55, 73, 98, 134, 242*

🚆 *Charing Cross*

Ⓟ *Drury Lane/Museum Street*

✶ *Air Condition*   ◁ *Infra-red*

♿ *Box*

☆ *Dress Circle bar is in a Jacobean style with oak panelling and wrought iron.*
The Theatre now known as the Shaftesbury opened in 1911 as the New
Prince's Theatre, dropping the New in 1914, before assuming its current
title in 1963. Designed by Bertie Crew, its stone exterior is Modern
Renaissance style with a tower above the corner entrance. The auditorium is considered to be one of the most beautiful in London, with
French wedding cake style plasterwork in pink and white. Seated life-
size classical figures, representing Comedy, Tragedy, Poetry and Music,
surmount the boxes, which are supported by Ionic columns. Conceived
as a home for melodrama at popular prices, its intimate feel coupled
with a large seating capacity makes it suitable for everything from drama
to opera and ballet. From the start its fare was eclectic, encompassing
romantic opera such as *Monsieur Beaucaire* (1919), Sarah Bernhardt's final
London performance as *Daniel* (1921), Diaghalev's Russian Ballet (1921
and 1927), *Macbeth* with Sybil Thorndyke (1926) and *Funny Face* with
Fred and Adele Astair (1928). At various points in its history, the
Shaftesbury has provided a temporary venue for other theatres' compa-
nies – the D'Oyly Carte Opera company performed here in 1919,
Sadler's Wells opera and ballet in 1944, and it was one of the theatres
used by the Royal Opera when Covent Garden was closed in 1998.
Since World War II it has mostly been home to musicals with *Pal Joey*
(1954), *Wonderful Town* (1955), *How To Succeed In Business Without Really
Trying* (1963), Lionel Bart's notorious flop *Twang!* (1965), *Follies* (1987),
Kiss Of The Spider Woman (1992), *Carousel* (1993), *Tommy* (1996) and
Rent (1998). The most controversial was *Hair* (1968) 'the tribal love rock
musical' which delayed its opening until the day after the abolition of
theatre censorship, and made good use of it by bringing nudity to the
London stage. In 1973 just short of its 2000th performance part of the
auditorium ceiling collapsed bringing an end to the run, and many
people thought the theatre, but it was eventually listed, repaired and
reopened in 1974. In 1984 The Theatre Of Comedy Company acquired
it and staged a mixture of new works and classics including See How
They Run (1984), *Pygmalion* (1984) and *An Italian Straw Hat* (1986).

Shaftesbury

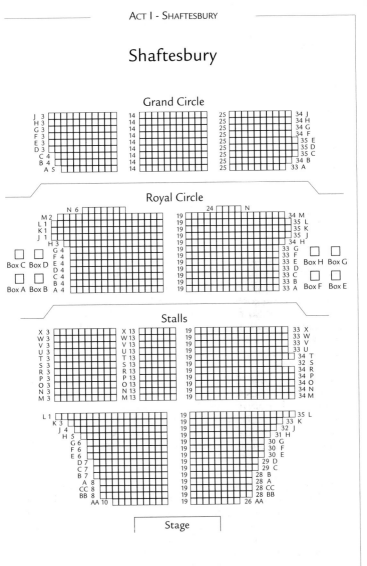

Grand Circle

Royal Circle

Stalls

Stage

60▲ Upper Circle, 0▲ Dress Circle, 22▼ Stalls, 1▲ Foyer, 🕃 1408

135

Shakespeare's Globe

⌨ *New Globe Walk, SE1 9DT*
☎ *020 7401 9919*
✎ *www.shakespeares-globe.org*
⊖ *Blackfriars / London Bridge / Southwark*
🚌 *45, 63, 344, 381*
🚆 *London Bridge / Blackfriars* Ⓟ *Upper Thames Street / On street*
✦ *Completely* ⤙ *Induction Loop*
♿ *Yard*
☆ *Performances May to September but exhibition, restaurant and bookshop open all year round*

Shakespeare's Globe

The first public playhouse in London was The Theatre, constructed outside the city wall to the north in Shoreditch in 1576, and managed by the actor James Burbage. It was in the form now familiar to us through the film Shakespeare In Love, with half the audience standing in the open air yard below the stage and the rest seated under cover in three shallow galleries surrounding them. The Theatre was so successful that Burbage built another, The Curtain, nearby the following year. A rival company run by Philip Henslowe built The Rose in 1587 on the south side of the river in Bankside. This was a rough area famous for entertainments such as cock fighting, bear baiting and bare knuckle boxing matches. In 1594 The Swan was built by Francis Langley at the west end of Bankside. By this time each of the theatres had a resident dramatist. Shakespeare arrived in London in the 1580s and began to work at The Theatre. When James Burgbage died in 1597 his sons Richard and Cuthburt were unable to renew the lease on the land where The Theatre stood. Their response was to dismantle the building, transport it across the river and erect it in Bankside near the others, and rechristen it The Globe. Its first recorded performance was *Julius Caesar* on 21st September 1599 and it became the most famous of London's theatres, presenting Shakespeare's plays, with Richard Burbage creating many of the leading roles. In 1613 during a performance of *Henry VIII* the Globe burned down after sparks from a cannon set the thatched roof alight. It was immediately rebuilt, and continued in operation until all theatres were closed by the Puritans in 1642, after which it was demolished in 1644. American actor Sam Wanamaker had a dream to rebuild the Globe as authentically as possible in Bankside and he set up a trust to raise the finance to do so in 1970. As no plans or drawings existed, the exact details of its construction and location were not known, so considerable research was needed before the design by Theo Crosby could be finalised. After a Herculean struggle Wanamaker managed to secure a site and raise the construction costs. Building began in 1987 and was completed in 1997. Sadly Wanamaker died in 1993 with little more than half of the main structure complete. The foundations of the original Globe were discovered in 1989 about 200 yards from the current building. Plays by Shakespeare and his contemporaries are performed as authentically as possible. Actors wear period underwear beneath their costumes, Mark Rylance played Cleopatra in 1998, performances are given in the afternoons, and in the evenings with simulated daylight, audience participation by those standing in the yard is encouraged – and they still fire the cannon.

Shakespeare's Globe

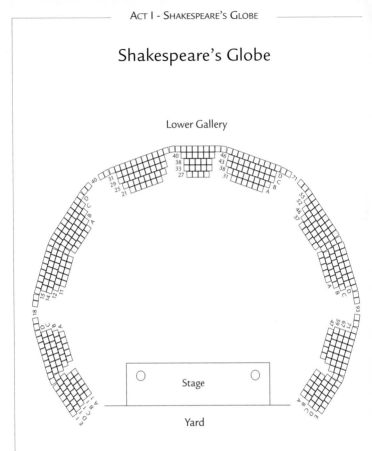

Lower Gallery

Stage

Yard

50▲ Upper Circle, 28▲ Dress Circle, 4▲ Stalls Circle, 0▲ Yard
0▲ Foyer, ♿ 881+600 standing in open Yard

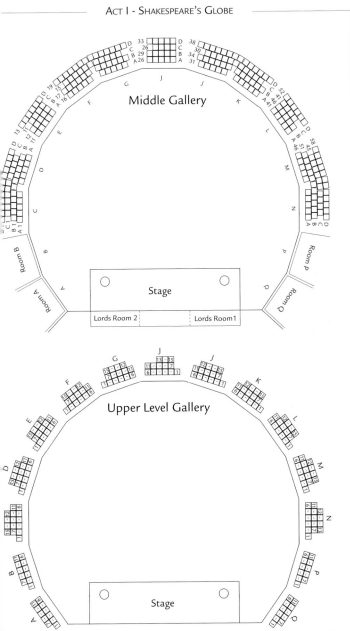

Strand

⌨ *The Aldwych, WC2B 5LD*

☎ *020 7930 8800*

⊖ *Covent Garden/Holborn/Temple*

🚌 *1, 4, 6, 9, 11, 13, 15, 23, 26, 59, 68, 76, 77A, 91, 168, 171, 172,*

🚆 *Charing Cross*

Ⓟ *Drury Lane/Bedfordbury*

♿ *Dress Circle*

☆ *Putti cherubs above the boxes in the auditorium*

Designed by W G R Sprague as a twin to the Aldwych, with which it bookends the block, the Strand was the first to open in 1905 as the Waldorf Theatre, although its name changed to the Strand in 1909, the Whitney in 1911 and back to the Strand in 1913. It has a classical façade in Portland stone with pediments and columns almost identical to those of the Aldwych, but with statues in front of the central columns on its top level. The Louis XIV style interior is more lavish, with figures holding lamps at the foot of the staircase in the foyer leading to the auditorium, where the boxes are framed with marble Ionic pillars and surmounted by cupids. Above the proscenium is a bas-relief of Apollo in a chariot pulled by four horses, attended by goddesses and cupids, and on the ceiling there are allegorical figures painted after Le Brun. It received minor bomb damage in both World Wars, during performances by Fred Terry and Donald Wolfit respectively, which on neither occasion were abandoned. It opened with a programme alternating opera and plays in Italian with Elenora Duse and her company. Most of the great names of the time appeared here, including H B Irving in *Lights Out* (1905) and Herbert Beerbohm Tree in *Oliver Twist* (1905). The Strand saw the British premiere of Chekhov's *The Cherry Orchard* (1909) and *Treasure Island* was a regular Christmas visitor from 1922 to 1926. Mirroring the Aldwych farces came *It's A Boy!* (1930), *It's A Girl!* and *Night Of The Garter* (1932), *1066 And All That* (1935), and then the Aldwych company moved in with *Aren't Men Beasts* (1936), *A Spot Of Bother* (1937), *Banana Ridge* (1938) and *Spotted Dick* (1939). *Arsenic And Old Lace* (1942) was the theatre's longest running show until *Sailor Beware* (1955) made a star of Peggy Mount. A record subsequently broken by the 11 year run of *No Sex Please – We're British!* (1971), which made a star of Michael Crawford. Frankie Howerd found the part of a lifetime as the put upon Roman slave in *A Funny Thing Happened On The Way To The Forum* (1963). Important premieres in recent years include Tom Stoppard's *The Real Thing* (1982), David Mamet's *A Life In The Theatre* (1989) and Alan Ayckbourn's *The Revenger's Comedies* (1991).

Strand

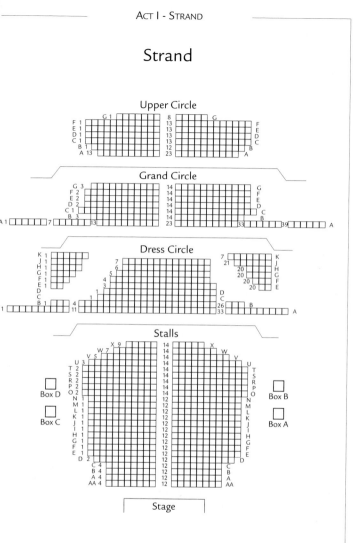

70▲ Balcony, 40▲ Upper Circle, 7▲ Dress Circle, 32▼ Stalls
8▲ Foyer, 🏛 1067

Vaudeville

- 🏠 *The Strand, WC2R 0NH*
- ☎ *020 7836 9987*
- ⊖ *Charing Cross/Covent Garden/Leicester Square*
- 🚌 *6, 9, 11, 13, 15, 23, 77A, 91, 176*
- 🚃 *Charing Cross*
- Ⓟ *Bedfordbury/Trafalgar Square*
- ✈ *Air Condition*
- ☆ *Bust of Shakespeare in a mirrored niche in the Dress Circle foyer*

When the first theatre designed by C J Phipps opened here in 1870, the existing buildings on the Strand were retained and an entrance made through one of them. In 1891 the interior was modified and the present façade of Portland stone, with a first floor loggia and casement windows looking like a private house, was constructed. In 1926 the façade was retained when the interior was gutted and replaced with a design by Robert Atkinson. This eliminated curves, replacing the auditorium's horseshoe shape with a rectangle, but retained some of Phipps' classical ornamentation. Henry Irving made his name here in *The Two Roses* (1870). *Our Boys* (1875) broke all previous London records with a four year run, and was followed by *Our Girls* (1879). Ibsen's *Romersholm* and *Hedda Gabler* both received their first British performances in 1891. The next years saw light comedies featuring actor managers Seymour Hicks and wife Ellaline Terriss, and Charles Hawtrey. For ten years André Charlot presented a series of revues starting with *Samples* (1915), *Some* (1916), *Cheep* (1917), *Tabs* (1918), *Buzz-Buzz* (1918) which broke previous revue records through to *Yes* (1923) with Beatrice Lillie. After reconstruction revue returned with *RSVP* and continued for another ten years, including *Charlot's Non-Stop Revue* (1937) after which another refurbishment took place. The comedy *The Chiltern Hundreds* (1947) launched the career of playwright William Douglas Home (returning in 2000) and in 1954 the record breaking musical *Salad Days* (1954) did the same for Julian Slade and Dorothy Reynolds (returning in 1995). It was after a matinée performance of the original production that a young boy called Cameron Mackintosh demanded to go backstage to find out how the magic piano worked. Thus was the course British musical theatre history transformed. For the Slade/Reynolds team however lightning did not strike again with *Follow That Girl* (1960) or *Wildest Dreams* (1961). Theatre taste had moved on to Arnold Wesker's *Chips With Everything* (1962). Similarly farce, in the shape of *The Man Most Likely To …* (1968) with Leslie Phillips and *Move Over Mrs Markham* (1971) with Moira Lister, gave way to Alan Ayckbourn's *Absurd Person Singular* (1973), *Woman In Mind* (1987), *Henceforward* (1989) and *Time Of My Life* (1993), Willy Russell's *Shirley Valentine* (1988) with Pauline Collins, and Terry Johnson's *Dead Funny* (1994).

Vaudeville

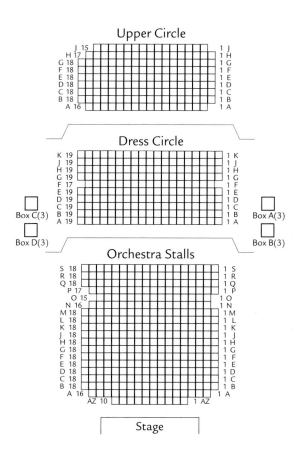

Upper Circle

J 15   1 J
H 17   1 H
G 18   1 G
F 18   1 F
E 18   1 E
D 18   1 D
C 18   1 C
B 18   1 B
A 16   1 A

Dress Circle

K 19   1 K
J 19   1 J
H 19   1 H
G 19   1 G
F 17   1 F
E 19   1 E
D 19   1 D
C 19   1 C
B 19   1 B
A 19   1 A

Box C(3)   Box A(3)
Box D(3)   Box B(3)

Orchestra Stalls

S 18   1 S
R 18   1 R
Q 18   1 Q
P 17   1 P
O 15   1 O
N 16   1 N
M 18   1 M
L 18   1 L
K 18   1 K
J 18   1 J
H 18   1 H
G 18   1 G
F 18   1 F
E 18   1 E
D 18   1 D
C 18   1 C
B 18   1 B
A 16   1 A
AZ 10   1 AZ

Stage

59▲ Upper Circle, 27▲ Dress Circle, 5▼ Stalls, 0▲ Foyer, ♿ 690

143

Victoria Palace

⌨ *Victoria Street, SW1E 5EA*

☎ *020 834 1317*

⊖ *Victoria*

🚌 *2, 8, 11, 16, 24, 36, 38, 52, 73, 82, 185, 239, 507, C1, C10*

🚃 *Victoria*

Ⓟ *Rochester Row/Vauxhall Bridge Road*

✈ *Air Condition* ⤶ *Infra-red & Induction Loop*

♿ *Stalls*

☆ *The centre of the dome in the auditorium ceiling slides open for increased ventilation*

Built on the site of Moy's Music Hall (later the Royal Standard), which was the first premises in London to hold a music hall license, Victoria Palace was designed by Frank Matcham and opened in 1911. It has a classical white patent stone façade, with a third floor loggia of Ionic columns, surmounted with a Baroque tower crowned with a dome. A mosaic above the entrance depicts two figures, one holding a lyre, the other a mask. Originally a gilded statue of Pavlova graced the tower, but this was removed during World War II. The theatre was built at the height of the music hall boom and owner Alfred Butt wanted it to compete with the best. Although the auditorium is narrower, the interior bears some resemblance to the London Palladium, richly furnished and gilded with Sicilian marble pillars. It opened with variety, and all the best-known names of the period appeared here, joined each Christmas by a fairy play *The Windmill Man* (1921-31). Eventually it moved over to revue with Gracie Fields in *The Show's The Thing* (1929). In 1934 a curiosity called *Young England* became a huge and unlikely hit for the theatre. Written by 84 year old Walter Reynolds as a serious patriotic drama, its melodramatic tale of a scoutmaster unjustly accused of pilfering the scout funds was received as a comedy, with audiences cheering and jeering as the plot unfolded. The management was forced to employ 'chuckers-out' to deal with over excited members of the audience. Other dramas were tried unsuccessfully before its first real hit with Lupino Lane in the musical *Me And My Girl* (1937) which returned in 1944. The Crazy Gang transferred here from the Palladium with *Together Again* (1947), *Knights Of Madness* (1950), *Ring Out The Bells* (1952), *Jokers Wild* (1954), *Crown Jewels* (1959), and their farewell appearance *Young In Heart* (1960). *The Black And White Minstrel Show* (1962), a stage version of the television series, was succeeded by *The Magic Of The Minstrels* (1970), which ran for ten years. It became a musical house with *Annie* (1978), and has since seen *Windy City* (1982), *High Society* (1987), and *Buddy* (1989) plus a number of notorious flops. Elizabeth Taylor made her London stage debut here in Lillian Hellman's *The Little Foxes* (1982), which was more a curiosity than a drama.

Victoria Palace

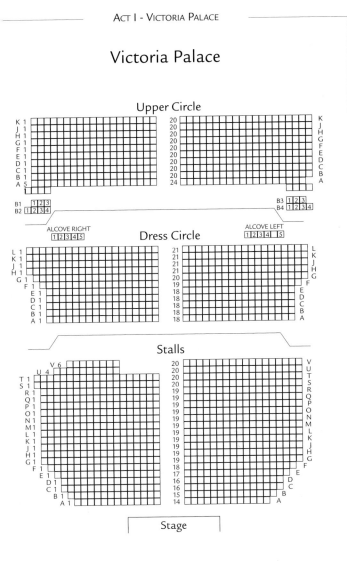

Upper Circle

Dress Circle

ALCOVE RIGHT
1 2 3 4 5

ALCOVE LEFT
1 2 3 4 5

Stalls

Stage

75 ▲ Upper Circle, 28 ▲ Dress Circle, 4 ▼ Stalls, 0 ▲ Foyer, 🏛 *1554*

Whitehall

⌨ *Whitehall, SW1Y 2DYR*
☎ *020 7369 1735*
✆ *www.theambassadors.com*
⊖ *Charing Cross/Embankment*
🚌 *3, 11, 12, 24, 53, 77A, 88, 159*
🚃 *Charing Cross*
Ⓟ *Trafalgar Square/Whitcomb Street*
✈ *Air Condition*
☆ *Splendid Art Deco design details in the auditorium*

Built on the site of Ye Old Ship Tavern, which dated from 1650, it was designed by Edward A Stone, with an interior by French designers Marc-Henri Levy and Gaston Laverdet and opened in 1930. The simple exterior of plain white Portland stone has a temple-like quality that makes a stylistic nod towards the Cenotaph further down Whitehall. In complete contrast the interior is possibly the best example of Art Deco theatre design anywhere. Black walls – the first such use in Britain – are decorated with silver hatching and floral designs in pastel shades, together with musical instrument and mask motifs in gold, and cubist panels at the sides of the auditorium. It has been best known for two things – flesh and farce. Phyllis Dixey was the West End's first stripper in non-stop revues *Whitehall Follies* (1942) and *Good Night Ladies* (1944) creating the art of 'ecdysism' (as Gypsy Rose Lee called it) talking to the audience as she disrobed. To comply with licensing regulations she had to remain stationary once naked. The flesh era returned after the abolition of censorship, with *Pyjama Tops* (1969), an innocuous comedy into which female nudity was gratuitously (and profitably) injected, and again less successfully with Fem 2 Fem in the so-called musical *Voyeurz* (1996). Farce however has been the Whitehall's staple, starting with *Worms Eye View* (1945) with Ronald Shiner and Brian Rix playing a northerner always losing his trousers. Rix went on to produce and often star in *Reluctant Heroes* (1950), *Dry Rot* (1954), *Simple Spyman* (1958), *One For The Pot* (1961), *Chase Me Comrade* (1964) and *Uproar In The House* (1967). During the longest run of continuous production by one management in one theatre, Rix launched the writing careers of actors John Chapman and Ray Cooney. In the late 1970s its unauthorised use as a museum of war memorabilia was ended by a public enquiry. The Whitehall was refurbished and restored to its original splendour, reopening in 1985 with J B Priestley's *When We Are Married*. Unusual shows which have played here include John Wells' political comedy *Anyone For D* (1982) based on the Private Eye magazine column, drag act Hinge And Bracket in *The Importance Of Being Earnest* (1987) and *Rick's Bar Casablanca* (1991), the play on which the film was based.

Whitehall

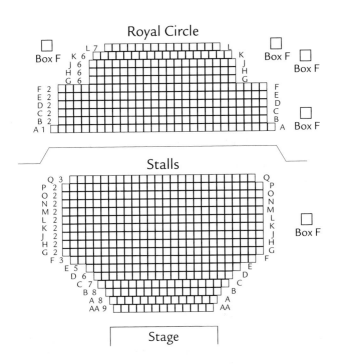

Royal Circle

Box F

Box F

Box F

Box F

L 7   L
K 6   K
J 6   J
H 6   H
G 6   G
F 2   F
E 2   E
D 2   D
C 2   C
B 2   B
A 1   A

Stalls

Box F

Q 3   Q
P 2   P
O 2   O
N 2   N
M 2   M
L 2   L
K 2   K
J 2   J
H 2   H
G 2   G
F 3   F
E 5   E
D 6   D
C 7   C
B 8   B
A 8   A
AA 9   AA

Stage

14▲ Dress Circle, 25▼ Stalls, 1▲ Foyer, 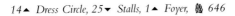 *646*

147

Wyndham's

- ⌨ *Charing Cross Road, WC2H 0DA*
- ☎ *020 7369 1736*
- ✎ *www.theambassadors.com*
- ⊖ *Leicester Square*
- 🚌 *24, 29, 176*
- 🚆 *Charing Cross*
- Ⓟ *Lisle Street/Upper St Martin's Lane*
- ✈ *Air Condition* ◁ *Infra-red*
- ☆ *The house tabs are a fine example of the extravagant Victorian style*

Actor manager Charles Wyndham purchased the site from Lord Salisbury after his leading lady and wife Mary Moore had managed to find ten friends to stand guarantors of a £1000 loan each. The first theatre designed by W G R Sprague, it was built on one half of the land in Charing Cross Road and opened in 1899. The Albery in St Martin's Lane, also by Sprague as his first twin, followed in 1903. Both have similar French classical façades with arched balconied windows. The interior is in Louis XVI style in cream, pale blue and gold, with the monograms CW and MM much in evidence. The proscenium is a complete four sided picture frame, above which are two angels holding portraits of Sheridan and Goldsmith in front of a gold winged bust, thought to be of Mary Moore. The ceiling is decorated with Boucher inspired paintings of pastoral scenes. The well-made play has been its trademark starting with Wyndham in *Cyrano de Begerac* and *Mrs Dane's Defence* (1900), and J M Barrie's *Little Mary* (1903). *An Englishman's Home* (1909) written anonymously by 'A Patriot' (actually Gerald du Maurier's brother Guy) about an invasion of England caused a stir and prompted an increase in recruitment in the Territorial Army during pre World War I fervour. Gerald du Maurier appeared in *Raffles* (1914), *Dear Brutus* (1917), *The Choice* (1919), *Bulldog Drummond* (1921) and with Tallulah Bankhead making her London debut in *The Dancers* (1923). Edgar Wallace had an apartment here while his crime dramas were presented, from *The Ringer* (1926), through *Smokey Cell* (1930) when the audience were asked to believe they were to watch an execution by electric chair being given reproduction journalists cards instead of tickets, to *The Green Pack* (1932). Transfers provided many successes including the Players' unexpected hit musical *The Boy Friend* (1954), Joan Littlewood's Theatre Workshop's *A Taste Of Honey* and *The Hostage* (1959) and *Oh, What A Lovely War* (1963), and from the Arts *Entertaining Mr Sloane* (1964), the Roundhouse *Godspell* (1972), and the National Theatre Harold Pinter's *No Man's Land* (1975) with John Gielgud and Ralph Richardson. Contemporary plays that made a mark were Peter Nichols *Passion Play* (1984), Caryl Churchill's *Serious Money* (1987), David Hare's *Skylight* (1996), and *Art* (1996).

Wyndham's

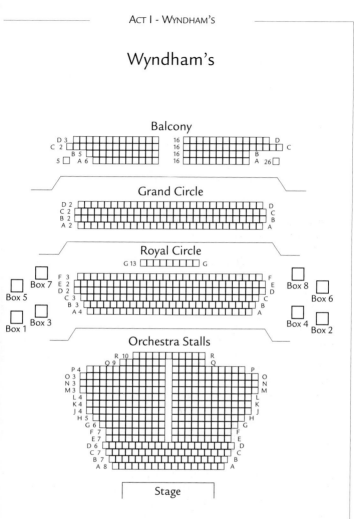

Balcony

D 3
C 2
B 5
5 □ A 6

16
16
16
16

D
C
B
A 26 □

Grand Circle

D 2
C 2
B 2
A 2

D
C
B
A

Royal Circle

G 13   G

Box 5   Box 7

F 3
E 2
D 2
C 3
B 3
A 4

F
E
D
C
B
A

Box 8   Box 6

Box 1   Box 3

Box 4   Box 2

Orchestra Stalls

R 10
Q 9
P 4
O 3
N 3
M 3
L 4
K 4
J 4
H 5
G 6
F 7
E 7
D 6
C 7
B 7
A 8

R
Q
P
O
N
M
L
K
J
H
G
F
E
D
C
B
A

Stage

43▲ Balcony, 21▲ Upper Circle, 12▲ Dress Circle,
18▼ Stalls, 1▲ Foyer,  *759*

149

Carpet Fitter, Theatre Royal Drury Lane

OTHER VENUES

Theatres Beyond The West End

Almeida
🖃 *Almeida Street, Islington, N1 1TA*
☎ *020 7359 4404*
🖊 *www.almeida.co.uk*
The Almeida is currently located at a temporary site in King's Cross, while the Almeida site is redeveloped. Work should be completed in December 2002.

Greenwich
🖃 *Crooms Hill, Greenwich, SE10 8ES*
☎ *020 8858 7755*
🖊 *www.greenwichtheatre.org.uk*

Hackney Empire
🖃 *291 Mare Street, Hackney, E8 1EJ*
☎ *020 8985 2424*
🖊 *www.hackneyempire.co.uk*

Hampstead
🖃 *Swiss Cottage Centre, NW3 3EX*
☎ *020 7722 9301*
🖊 *www.hampstead-theatre.co.uk*

London Apollo
🖃 *Queen Caroline Street, Hammersmith, W6 9QH*
☎ *0870 606 3580*
🖊 *www.apollo-leisure.co.uk*

Lyric Hammersmith
🖃 *King Street, Hammersmith, W6 0QL*
☎ *020 8741 2311*
🖊 *www.lyric.co.uk*

Richmond
🖃 *The Green, Richmond, TW9 1QJ*
☎ *020 8940 0088*
🖊 *www.theambassadors.com/richmond*

Theatre Royal Stratford East
- *Theatre Square, Stratford, E15 1BN*
- *020 8534 0310*
- *www.stratfordeast.com*

Tricycle
- *269 Kilburn High Road, NW6 7JR*
- *020 7328 1000*
- *www.tricycle.co.uk*

Wimbledon
- *The Broadway, Wimbledon, SW19 1QG*
- *020 8540 0362*
- *213.86.36.4/info/wimbledon.htm*

Young Vic
- *66 The Cut, SE1 8LZ*
- *020 7928 6363*
- *www.youngvic.org*

Fringe Theatres

Battersea Arts Centre
- *Old Town Hall, Lavender Hill, Battersea, SW11 5TF*
- *020 7223 2223*
- *www.bac.org.uk*

Bridewell
- *Bride Lane (Off Fleet Street), EC4Y 8EQ*
- *0207 936 3456*
- *www.bridewelltheatre.co.uk*

Bush
- *Shepherd's Bush Green, W12 8QD*
- *020 8743 3388*
- *www.bushtheatre.co.uk*

Cochrane
- *Southampton Row, WC1B 4AP*
- *020 7242 7040*

The Drill Hall
- *16 Chenies Street, WC1E 7EX*
- *020 7637 8270*

Jermyn Street

⌨ *168 Jermyn Street, SW1Y 6ST*
☎ *020 7287 2875*
✍ *www.jermynstreettheatre.co.uk*

King's Head

⌨ *115 Upper Street, Islington, N1 1QN*
☎ *020 7226 1916*

New End

⌨ *27 New End, Hampstead, NW3 1JD*
☎ *020 7794 0022*

Orange Tree

⌨ *1 Clarence Street, Richmond, TW9 2SA*
☎ *020 8940 3633*

The Place

⌨ *17 Duke's Road, WC1H 9AB*
☎ *020 7387 0031*
✍ *www.theplace.org.uk*

Pleasance London

⌨ *Carpenters Mews, North Road, Lower Holloway, N7 9EF*
☎ *020 7609 1800*
✍ *www.pleasance.co.uk*

Riverside Studios

⌨ *Crisp Road, Hammersmith, W6 9RL*
☎ *020 8237 1111*
✍ *www.riversidestudios.co.uk*

Soho

⌨ *21 Dean Street, W1V 6NE*
☎ *020 7287 5060*
✍ *www.sohotheatre.com*

Specialist Theatres

Little Angel

⌨ *14 Dagmar Passage, Cross Street, Islington N1 2DN*
☎ *020 7226 1787*
✍ *www.littleangeltheatre.co.uk*
Home of British puppetry

Polka

⌨ *240 The Broadway, SW19 1SB*
☎ *020 8543 4888*
✎ *www.polkatheatre.com*
Children's plays and musicals

Players'

⌨ *The Arches (Off Villiers Street), WC2N 6NG*
☎ *020 7839 1134*
✎ *www.theplayerstheatre.co.uk*
Victorian Music Hall

Concert Halls

Barbican Hall

⌨ *Silk Street, EC2Y 8DS*
☎ *020 7638 8891*
✎ *www.barbican.org.uk*

Royal Albert Hall

⌨ *Kensington Gore, SW7 2AP*
☎ *020 7823 7725*
✎ *www.royalalberthall.com*

St John's Smith Square

⌨ *Smith Square, SW1P 3HA*
☎ *020 7222 1061*
✎ *www.sjss.org.uk*

Royal Festival Hall (Queen Elizabeth Hall, Purcell Room)

⌨ *South Bank SE1 8XX*
☎ *020 7960 4242*
✎ *www.rfh.org.uk*

Wigmore Hall

⌨ *36 Wigmore Street, W1H 0BP*
☎ *020 7935 2141*
✎ *www.wigmore-hall.org.uk*

ACT II - THE BOOKING

2.1 How To Book
Box Office, House Seats and Returns, Disabilities, Parking, Ticket Agents.

2.2 Where To Sit
Different levels of the theatre explained.

2.3 Discounts and Special Offers
Standbys, Ticket Booth, Show Pairs, ShowSavers, Upgrades, Free, Extras.

2.4 Education and Youth Programmes
School and teacher programmes, Masterclasses, Kids Week, Workshops, Kids Clubs.

2.5 Sources of Information
Free, Paid for journals, Websites.

2.6 Ticket Sales Agents
Box Offices, Ticket Agents – Phone/Online – Group Bookings – Theatre Breaks.

Lyric Theatre, Door Detail

HOW TO BOOK

Box Office

Your first port of call should always be the theatre Box Office, either in person, by phone, fax or online. It will have the widest selection of tickets available at the cheapest price. Any ticket booked through a third party will have a service charge of some sort added to the ticket price.

It has never been easier to buy tickets than it is today. Most theatre Box Offices now offer a 24hr/7day telephone credit card service, so you can call from anywhere in the world at a cheap rate. You can charge tickets to your card, and if there is time they will be posted to you, if not you can collect them at the theatre on the night. Do arrive in plenty of time as there may be a queue, and you will need to bring the credit card with you and sign a receipt. Some theatres may charge a service fee for using a card but will advise you of this at the time of the booking.

You can also reserve tickets by phone (usually for 3 days) and send payment by cheque, postal order or theatre tokens, enclosing a stamped addressed envelope, or pay in person at the theatre. Tickets will not normally be held until the day of performance unless paid for.

Most ticket agents, and resident companies such as the Barbican and Royal National Theatre, will now accept credit card bookings by fax. You will receive a faxed confirmation of your booking, and the tickets will be posted out or held for collection.

Some theatres now offer online ticketing. You can search their availability live, enter your credit card details and complete the transaction, although you will not be given seat numbers. Tickets will be posted out or held for collection. Some operate what is technically an email postal booking. You will be asked to fill in a form with your requirements and credit card details, and email it to the theatre. They will fulfil your request and email you confirmation. Again tickets will be posted out or held for collection.

There was originally no advance booking or numbered seats and each part of the theatre had a separate entrance. Audiences simply paid on arrival and sat where they liked within the level. The first tickets with numbers on were introduced in 1884. In Victorian times producers believed in large crowds at low prices, hence theatres were bigger and audiences crammed in. They also offered a wider price range and the difference between the cheapest and the most expensive seats was much greater than today. To sit in the Gallery then cost one sixth of the price of a seat in the Dress Circle, whereas today it is more like one third.

Box Offices are generally open to personal callers from 10.00am until 8.00pm or the start of the evening performance. You can usually pay by Sterling cash, credit card, debit card, Sterling cheque (supported by a guarantee card), Sterling traveller's cheques or theatre tokens.

Theatre tokens, which are exchangeable at all London theatres, can be purchased at Box Offices, major bookshop chains, or by credit card from the Society Of London Theatre web site or the 24hr Tokenline.

Unless there is a performance Box Offices are closed on Sundays. On Bank Holidays opening times may vary and there may even be no performance. If booking for future performances, it is always best to avoid the half hour immediately before a performance starts, both at matinées and evenings. The windows will be very busy with people collecting tickets, and so you may have to wait.

Box Office staff will offer you the best seats available at the time of your booking. Customers' latent persecution complexes often reveal themselves at this point, with an involuntary response of the dreaded phrase "Haven't you got anything more central?". In order to avoid initiating an ugly scene, remember that box office staff are not out to get you, but to do the best they can for you. As with all conspiracy theories, the truth is much simpler and duller.

Bear in mind what Box Office staff have to contend with. I once took part in the following exchange: Customer: "What time does it start?" Me: "7.30pm" Customer: "And the Dress Circle?"

Performances are generally Mondays to Saturdays, with matinées midweek on a Tuesday, Wednesday or Thursday, and on Saturday. Sunday performances have not really taken off in London, and there are rarely more than one or two shows that have substituted a Sunday matinée for Monday night. Evening performances generally start between 7.30pm and 8.00pm. Before World War II shows started later as in European countries – hence Noel Coward's one act play programmes *Tonight At 8.30*. The three auditoria of the National Theatre stagger their starting times at 7.15pm, 7.30pm and 7.45pm to spread the crush. Matinées generally commence between 2.30pm and 3.00pm, although occasionally Saturday matinées may start between 4.00pm and 5.00pm. With skilful planning and a pair of trainers you can sometimes fit in three shows in one day.

House Seats & Returns

Contrary to popular opinion, apart from *The Lion King* and *Mamma Mia!*, there are seats available for most West End shows on Mondays to Thursdays from the Box Office on the day of performance. Of course if you want front row centre Dress Circle on Saturday night you will need to book ahead – some months in the case of the big musicals.

Star Tip: Good seats usually go on sale on the day of the performance, as the Producer's House Seats are released and unsold ticket agents allocations are marked back. This usually happens either as the Box Office opens at 10.00am or at around 11.00 am. Sometimes these seats are available by phone, but on Saturdays and for shows that are almost sold out these may be restricted to sales at the Box Office window. It is always worth trying at the theatre in person if you can. The Royal National Theatre and the Royal Shakespeare Company hold some tickets back for sale on the day at the theatre only.

There is a faxback service providing seating availability information for the current day's performance. Just dial 09069 111 311 from the handset or keypad of your fax machine. This is a premium rate service, costing £1 per minute, and lasting approximately two minutes.

At sold out performances there is usually a queue for returns. These are tickets which people have bought previously but are unable to use, and ask the Box Office to resell on their behalf. For the big shows seats are often purchased months in advance, and ticket holders die or emigrate before they mature. There is an apocryphal story of the first ever empty seat at a matinee of the original production of *My Fair Lady*, which had been standing room only for months. The manager asks the lady next to it if she knows why it is unoccupied. Woman: "I booked the tickets nine months ago for my husband and I, but unfortunately he has since died." Manager: "Couldn't anyone else from you family have come with you?" Woman: "Oh no – they're all at the funeral."

The queue for returns usually starts about 1-2 hours before the performance (although for *The Lion King* and *Mamma Mia!* it's 3-4 hours). Tickets must be paid for in cash and may be restricted to one per person. Check with the Box Office for their policy.

Disabilities

If you have a disability, most theatres have a specialist to help with your needs when making a booking. Given that the majority of London theatres are listed Victorian or Edwardian buildings conditions are not ideal but they do the best they can. Some street level access is usually available, and seats can be removed to accommodate wheelchairs, but this must be requested when making a booking. Most theatres have either an infra-red or induction loop sound amplification system. Guide dogs are not generally allowed into the auditorium, but are willingly looked after by the front of house staff. Usually a reduced price is offered for yourself and an escort or carer, and an attendant will be assigned to assist.

Signed, audio described and subtitled performances are given regularly. Signed Performances In Theatre provides information on signed performances. Vocaleyes provides a programme of live audio described performances. Stagetext provides a programme of open-captioned performances. The Shape Ticket Scheme gives disabled and elderly people access to reduced price tickets, as well as providing transport and escorts to theatre and music events. There is a £10 annual membership fee, which includes a monthly newsletter. Tripscope offers information and help with organising transport for disabled or elderly people. Artsline provides an information and advice service for disabled people on London's arts and entertainment, as does the National Disability Arts Forum. Radar provides advice and information on general access.

A booklet detailing facilities, Access Guide To London's West End Theatres is published by the Society Of London Theatre and is available free at Box Offices or by post from SOLT. This information is also available on SOLT's web site, together with a listing of forthcoming signed, audio described and subtitled performances.

Parking

On street parking meters and single yellow line restrictions apply between 8.30am and 6.30pm Monday to Saturday throughout most of the West End (City of Westminster and Borough of Camden). Generally, after 6.30pm and at any time on Sunday, you may park free of charge on meters and on single yellow lines, but always check to be sure.

The West End Leisure Scheme offers reduced rate parking to theatre and cinemagoers at MasterPark car parks seven days a week. The rates are: Up to 5 hours for £5.00, Up to 7 hours for £7.50 and Up to 9 hours for £10. Present your ticket stub when paying. Car parks operating this scheme are situated at Cavendish Square, Marble Arch, Newport Place, Park Lane, Poland Street, Rochester Row, Spring Gardens and Whitcomb Street. The scheme is valid for customers arriving after 9am and leaving before midnight on the date of the performance only. For further information or a free car park map call 0800 243348.

Ticket Agents

Most major ticket agencies also offer a 24hr/7day telephone credit card service and/or online booking. The larger agencies have an allocation of seats at each performance, so that if the Box Office is sold out, they may be able to help you. If you book with an agent, they should tell you the face value of the ticket, the location of the seat, and if the view of the stage is restricted in any way. They will generally charge a service fee, but reputable agents will advise you of this at the time of booking, and it will not exceed 25%.

An alliance of reputable agents called STAR – Society of Ticket Agents and Retailers – works on a similar basis to the ABTA travel agents association. It has a code of conduct by which all its members must abide. You are strongly advised not to deal with anyone who is not a member.

Beware of ticket touts or scalpers. If you are not told the face value of the ticket, the location of the seat, and if the view of the stage is restricted in any way do not buy. Never buy from someone in the street, and beware of the proliferation of small outlets in the vicinity of the Leicester Square tkts-Official Half Price Ticket Booth, the clock tower pavilion centrally located in the southside of the Square. If you purchase the ticket in person, always make sure you have seen the ticket and the location on a seating plan before paying. It is not illegal to charge a service fee, but it is illegal to remove or change the face value on a ticket. Never pay for a ticket in person and arrange to collect it later from the theatre, unless you receive a printed agency voucher, with full company details, and the seat number and price on it.

I was once working in the Box Office of *The Phantom Of The Opera* when a Spanish couple came to the window with a sheet torn from a duplicate book on which was written "Seat two people" for which they had paid £200 to someone in the street. As the performance was sold out, including all the returns by the time of their arrival, sadly there was nothing we could do but turn them away.

Tickets purchased from an unauthorised dealer may be forged or stolen, in which case in addition to being overcharged, you will not be allowed into the theatre. If you feel that you have been misled by an agent please let the Society Of London Theatre know.

Her Majestys Theatre

161

WHERE TO SIT

The part of the theatre where the audience sits is the auditorium. Most London auditoria have three levels. Some have four and the Arts, Peacock and Prince of Wales have only two. The higher the level, the steeper the slope (or rake) of the seats to improve sightlines.

The lowest part, nearest the stage is the Stalls. Americans call it the Orchestra. The Stalls is the largest area of the auditorium. If you like to be close to the actors so you can see them 'warts and all', then this is for you. The rear half of the Stalls will be under the levels above, the overhang of which may restrict the view of the stage if the set is very tall. As set designers have grown to see their job as producing a "WOW!" from the expensive seats rather than a decent view from the cheap ones, this is inclined to happen more often than it used to.

Most London theatres were built before civil engineering reached the sophistication of cantilevering, thus there are often pillars to support the upper levels. Hence the music hall comedian's line "Don't clap too loud

Queens Theatre

's a very old building". The worst example is probably The Old Vic ith 17 pillars in three levels. Many theatres have four pillars repeated n each level. All seats deemed to offer a restricted view by the roducer are sold as such at a reduced rate. Experience may bring you) the conclusion that the first requirement of being a producer is an bility to see round corners.

he second level is the Dress Circle. Sometimes this is known as the oyal Circle because the Royal Box is on this level. Americans call it ie Balcony. This makes it easier for ticket touts to sell them tickets aarked Balcony (which is the fourth level and consequently the worst a the house) for a huge amount, because they think they are buying the est. Many people claim that the Dress Circle is the best place from hich to see a show – in a slightly elevated position looking down on ie actors.

he third level is the Upper Circle. Not to be confused with the upper lass, this is where the poor people sit. As Dame Edna Everage says: "I'm oing to look at you paupers just once because that's all you get for vhat you paid". These are the cheap seats (inasmuch as any are cheap owadays) – perhaps cheaper is more accurate. They are furthest away om the stage looking more steeply down. There is not much to be aid about this level, as there is often not much to be seen from it.

f there is one, the fourth level really is called the Balcony. Frequently iis has a separate entrance from the rest of the theatre. This dates back) when this level was called the Gallery, and seating here was unbook-ble unnumbered benches, sold on admission, with the soundest of wind nd limb racing up the stairs to claim the front row. It would be nice to nd that kind of commitment in audiences nowadays. The queue for eturns for *The Lion King* or *Mamma Mia!*, braving the rain and snow for iree hours is probably the only comparable thing in theatre today.

tar Tip: The view from the centre blocks of the Balcony at Her Aajesty's is very good value as it is not too high, since the theatre has nly half the capacity of most of the four level theatres.

he view from the Balcony of Drury Lane is the top of the actors eads, and mist or low cloud can be a problem. People who suffer from ertigo usually return ashen faced to the Box Office before the show has ven begun. To give some sense of scale, the Balcony of Drury Lane ontains more seats than the entire auditorium of the Fortune Theatre.

Until recently there were usually three ticket prices in the Stalls, depending on how close to the stage you were, and two in each of the Circles. This has now generally been reduced to one price per level, as on Broadway, with possibly the back row or two of the Stalls, which may be affected by the overhang of the Dress Circle, at a second price. Obviously the back row in the larger theatres cannot be as good a view as the front, so do check exactly where tickets are located when buying. Top price no longer guarantees best view.

On each level adjoining the stage there are usually Boxes, seating anything from 2 to 6 people. These are called "The Ash Trays" by comedians such as the one referred to earlier. Remember that Boxes were built to be seen in, rather than to see from. In a traditional Victorian horseshoe shaped auditorium they actually face slightly away from the stage. At best they offer a sideways on view, at worst they are restricted. Boxes are generally the same price as other seats, and each seat is sold individually – you only have the box to yourself if you pay for all of them. When you do have the Box exclusively if the performance is less than riveting you can misbehave in relative privacy. Do try not to disturb the actors though – a couple in a box at the Apollo ended up with more people watching them than the stage. Nowadays Boxes are often used for lighting and sound equipment, and so are not on sale.

When the London Palladium first opened, the quest for novelty saw a Box to Box telephone system installed. If patrons recognised friends in another Box across the auditorium they were able to engage them in conversation without the effort of walking all the way round.

At Dress Circle level and, access permitting, usually on the auditorium right, there is the Royal Box. This frequently has a separate entrance direct from the street so that the Monarch does not have to mix with the hoi polloi. The last word in Royal comfort was installed at the London Coliseum. An entire Royal Box was built on runners so that the Monarch could enter it direct from the street and glide into position in the auditorium. The first time it was called upon, to perform for Edward VII, it failed to work and has never been tried since. Adjoining the Royal Box is the Royal Retiring Room which allows the Monarch and their entourage to refresh themselves in private.

Not to be outdone by anyone else, Drury Lane effectively has two Royal Boxes, dating back to when George III and the Prince Of Wales were not on the best of terms. Having had an altercation on the stairs, in order that they didn't meet in future, they had a box each. The box

Queens Theatre, Opera Glasses for hire

the left of the theatre is the Royal Box, decorated with the royal coat arms, and on right the is the Prince Of Wales Box, decorated with the ince Of Wales feathers. Similarly the staircases leading from the foyer the Rotunda are still named the King's Side and the Prince's Side. eorge V knighted actor manager Frank Benson in the Royal Retiring oom at Drury Lane using a prop sword after a matinée of *Julius Caesar* 1916.

ecause of their age, restrictions of site, building regulations at the time construction and listed building status, London theatres may seem aint by current standards. Nevertheless they are masterpieces of ictorian or Edwardian ingenuity. In many theatres the Stalls is below ound level because of height restrictions when they were built – all e Shaftesbury Avenue theatres for instance. The exception is the New ondon which was built in the 1970s where the Stalls is at second floor vel with the foyer on the first floor approached by escalators. None ve lifts except the new Sadler's Wells, the refurbished Royal Opera ouse, and theatres that are part of a complex, such as the National and e Barbican. Be aware that climbing to the Balcony of Drury Lane is a at comparable to reaching the dome of St Paul's cathedral.

DISCOUNTS AND SPECIAL OFFERS

The days are past when producers could simply put the name of the show and its stars up on the marquee outside the theatre, and wait for people to beat a path to their door. Like all other businesses, theatres now have to sell themselves. This can work to the benefit of audiences as there are now a range of price options producers use which you can take advantage of.

On Mondays to Thursdays and for matinées there may be Standby reductions available for Students, Senior Citizens and Unemployed (UB40 holders). Generally these are any remaining best seats for about 1/3 of the normal price. These are usually available for cash only, from hour before the performance, one per person and are not bookable. Check with the Box Office for their policy.

tkts is the only official half price and discount theatre ticket booth in London. It is run by the Society Of London Theatre, and is centrally located in the clock tower pavilion on the south side of Leicester Square. Beware of imitators in the side roads around the Square. tkts offers tickets at half their face value, plus a service charge of £2.50, for wide range of shows on the day of performance only. Availability is posted on boards each day, and tkts opens Mondays to Saturdays from 10.00am to 7.00pm, and on Sundays from 12noon to 3.30pm. Paymen must be in cash or by credit card.

ShowPairs (see page 225) circulate special offers to businesses, posting out vouchers usually offering two seats for the price of one. There are various conditions applying which are printed on the vouchers. Ticket are only bookable direct with the Box Office, usually for Monday to Thursday performances and for a specific period of a month. The vouchers must be sent with payment or exchanged when tickets are collected. You can join the scheme for free, but remember offers are always subject to availability.

ShowSavers (see page 225) fax information overnight detailing last minute offers, sometimes with very big reductions for shows and concerts. There is also a ShowSavers On-line Club that posts these offers on the TheatreNet website, and circulates a weekly email Newsletter with a summary of the current deals. Again tickets must be booked direct with the Box Office, but a copy of the fax or email is no required. You can join the scheme for free, but remember offers are always subject to availability.

Ambassador Theatre Group's Upstage club entitles members to promotional discounts, a dedicated booking phone line, and free use of the Royal Retiring Room at their theatres. Annual membership costs £15.

The Royal National Theatre and English National Opera at the Coliseum offer some cheap tickets to personal callers at the Box Office only from 10.00am on the day of performance. These may be restricted to two per person. At the Royal Court Theatre and Soho Theatre all seats are £5 on Monday nights.

Star Tip: You may also be able to sit in the best seats at a cheaper price by strategic buying. Often at midweek matinées in less busy times of the year, Upper Circle and/or Balcony levels are closed and you will be reseated in the best seats. Alternatively you can buy restricted view seats and move to an empty full view seat as the house lights go down – or, if you are faint of heart, at the interval (Of course I didn't tell you that). Be careful to avoid half-term weeks when business shoots up.

Group reductions are usually available for Monday to Thursday performances and sometimes for Fridays and Saturdays. The minimum size of groups and prices vary so check with the Box Office. Some theatres have established a group booking office and send out regular newsletters with information and offers. Reservations can usually be held for up to four weeks. All ticket agents will handle group bookings, some make it their speciality.

Most shows play a week or so of previews before the press night, although sadly no longer at half-price. There are still some reductions, and they offer the extra excitement – and danger – of the show being played in. Adding the audience is the final element in creating a show, and until it happens no one knows quite how things will turn out. It is always interesting to make your own mind up before the critics see it.

Star Tip: If you want to be part of the first night, it is often possible to buy tickets a day or two beforehand, once the producer has allocated his requirements. There may be returns just before the show starts, and if the Box Office staff are feeling particularly kind-hearted they may even give away unused complementary tickets. Remember that first nights usually begin at 7.00pm.

If your interests embrace the arts generally, then The London Pass offers free entry to over 60 cultural institutions and visitor attractions, plus free travel via public transport, and discounts on certain theatre and cinema tickets. Available for 1, 2, 3 and 6 days.

Free

Each autumn the Society of London Theatre selects twelve enthusiastic and knowledgeable theatregoers to join one of the four judging panels for Britain's premier theatre awards - the Laurence Olivier Awards. Panellists receive a pair of free tickets for all shows playing in the West End during the following calendar year. Members of the theatre panel are expected to attend about 60 plays as well as musicals, dance and opera. Applications can be made online on the SOLT web site, or by filling out the form in the leaflets to be found in all West End theatres.

The National Theatre offers an extensive programme of events ranging from foyer music to platform productions and discussions, plus outdoor events in the Theatre Square in the summer months. Some of these events require booking and payment. Phone the National Theatre Box Office for further details about events.

The Barbican Centre has foyer music on weekdays from 5.30pm and Sundays from 12.30pm, plus talks, workshops and family events on Sundays. Again check with the Box Office for details.

The Royal Opera House stages chamber music concerts in the Linbury Studio on Mondays at 1.00pm. There are occasional free live relays of its performances of opera and ballet on a giant screen in the Covent Garden Piazza during the summer months. The Piazza is still the centre of street entertainment and you will find a miscellany of mime artists, jugglers and musicians at any time of the day or evening.

The Royal Festival Hall has foyer music of all kinds Wednesdays to Sundays from 12.30pm, jazz on Fridays from 5.15pm, plus outdoor events on the terraces in the summer months.

Churches that hold lunchtime recitals include St James' Piccadilly on Mondays, Wednesdays and Fridays at 1.10pm, St Martin-in-the-Fields on Mondays, Tuesdays and Fridays at 1.05pm, and Southwark Cathedral on Mondays and Tuesdays at 1.10pm

The main music colleges The Royal Academy of Music, Royal College of Music and Trinity College of Music, present a programme of lunchtime and evening concerts with a wide variety of music during term time.

Broadgate Circle in the city offers lunchtime and early evening music and entertainment events from May to September. The Broadgate Live monthly diary gives full details or call 020 7505 4000.

Canary Wharf in Docklands has an arts and events programme that runs throughout the year, outdoors in summer. Call 020 7418 2783.

Most of the Royal Parks – Green, Greenwich, Hyde, Regent's, Richmond and St James's, and Embankment and Kensington Gardens, have music and other events in the summer months. The Summer Entertainment Programme booklet gives full details, call 020 7298 2000.

Free tickets are available for recordings of radio and television programmes from the BBC and independent production companies (see page 196).

Extras

Royalty nowadays often sit in the Dress Circle rather than the Royal Box. As a result, the Royal Box and the Royal Retiring Room can be hired for VIP parties. So if you are planning an extra special night out, you can book a VIP package which will guarantee you the best seats, drinks and/or canapés in the Retiring Room before, during and/or after the show, your own attendant to minister to your needs, and free programmes and brochures. Packages are tailored to individual requirements.

If you have ever wondered how a theatre works, the following London theatres now offer backstage tours: Barbican Centre, Theatre Royal Drury Lane, Theatre Royal Haymarket, London Palladium, Royal National Theatre, New London, Royal Opera House, Sadler's Wells and Shakespeare's Globe. These generally last about an hour and a quarter, and run at regular times throughout the day Monday to Saturday – excluding matinée afternoons. Shakespeare's Globe and Theatre Royal Drury Lane tours also run on Sundays. Advance booking is recommended, as the size of groups is restricted. Young children are not admitted. These are working theatres and therefore access cannot be guaranteed to all areas of the buildings at all times.

You can now buy Theatre Break packages combining accommodation with tickets for shows and concerts. These can be tailored to individual requirements, with both midweek or weekend availability. Usually hotel prices are keener at the weekends, but tickets are cheaper and more readily available during the week. Again both the theatres themselves and agents who make it their speciality have a variety of packages available. It is worth shopping around.

EDUCATION & YOUTH PROGRAMMES

Many theatres now run education programmes in conjunction with their shows. These usually comprise project information packs for teachers for class work prior to the performance and special party rates for matinée and sometimes evening performances.

Really Useful Theatres' Class Act initiative offers a newsletter, a Teacher's Preview Programme to enable teachers to make informed decisions regarding productions for their pupils and school group rates for matinées and evening performances.

The Mousetrap Foundation provides free tickets for student-only performances of shows. Its Teacher's Preview Club offers teachers tickets at discounted prices, plus curriculum links, teaching resources, workshop programmes and a quarterly newsletter. There is also a Families First Night initiative to help families who could not normally afford tickets to see shows.

The Theatre Royal Haymarket holds regular seasons of Masterclasses for young people who have an interest in theatre, or are keen to pursue a career in the arts. They are open to people aged 16 and over, and are free of charge. All aspects of theatre production are covered with contributions by distinguished professionals from all fields. Tickets must be booked and confirmed in advance.

Kids Week in the West End organised by the Society Of London Theatre is designed to introduce young people to the theatregoing experience. Children between 5 and 16 can go free (when accompanied by a paying adult) to many West End shows, with up to two additional children at half-price. There is a programme of accompanying events including backstage tours, workshops and 'meet the cast' opportunities, plus discounts at restaurants, and on travel and accommodation packages. It takes place in the last week of August.

To cater for young adults there is Take A Date Or Bring A Mate, also organised by the SOLT, for people aged between 15 and 25. They can buy best available tickets for West End shows for £10. There is a maximum of two tickets per person and proof of age is required when collecting tickets from the box office. The offer takes place in the last week of January.

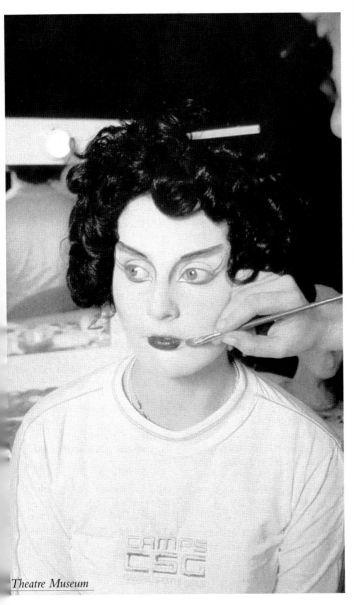

Theatre Museum

Kids Club In The West End is a co-operative venture by the Theatre Museum and the Society Of London Theatre designed to introduce young people to the theatregoing experience. 8 to 12 year olds are given a chance to explore famous shows through games and improvisation with West End professionals at the Theatre Museum on Saturday mornings. There are 15 places available each week, which are allocated on a first come first served basis. The Theatre Museum also runs regular make-up demonstrations, costume, shadow puppet and pantomime workshops.

The SOLT website has an Education section which includes details of special events, workshops, activities and inset training run by London theatres for schools and young people, together with special offers, and resources for teachers.

Although theatres make a positive attempt to welcome younger audiences, remember that infants under the age of 5 are not admitted to West End theatres.

SOURCES OF INFORMATION

Free
Most sources of general visitor information, as well as hotels will have flyers for West End shows.

The Official London Theatre Guide
www.OfficialLondonTheatre.co.uk
Free fortnightly guide produced by the Society Of London Theatre available at all West End theatres and information centres or posted to you on subscription.

London Planner
www.visitbritain.com
Free monthly guide produced by the British Tourist Authority with comprehensive entertainment listings available from hotels and information centres.

Footloose In London
Free weekly guide available at stands outside central underground and mainline railway stations.

Hot Tickets
Free weekly listings supplement with Evening Standard newspaper on Thursdays.

aid For Journals – available
n subscription

me Out

niverse House, 251 Tottenham Court
oad, W1P 0AB
l: 020 7813 3000
ix: 020 7813 6001
vw.timeout.com
eekly listings magazine.

'hat's On In London

30-182 Pentonville Road, N1 9LB
l: 020 7278 4393
ix: 020 7837 5838
vw.whatsoninlondon.co.uk
eekly listings magazine.

he Stage

7 Bermondsey Street, SE1 3XT
l: 020 7403 1818
ix: 020 7403 1418
vw.thestage.co.uk
eekly newspaper of the British
eatre.

heatre Record

05 Whitton Dene, Isleworth,
W7 7NE
l: 020 8737 8489
ix: 020 8893 9677
vw.theatrerecord.com
ortnightly magazine reproducing
l national newspaper reviews of
Vest End and regional shows.

elebrity Bulletin

ooms 203-209, 93-97
egent Street, W1R 7TA
l: 020 7439 9840
ix: 020 7494 3500
vw.celebritybulletin.com
wice weekly listing of celebrity

movements worldwide, including
the stars who are in London and
what they are doing.

Dance & Dancers

83 Clerkenwell Road, EC1R 5AR
Tel/Fax: 020 7813 1049
Monthly magazine with reviews
and features about British dance.

The Dancing Times

Clerkenwell House, 45-47
Clerkenwell Green, EC1R 0EB
Tel: 020 7250 3006
Fax: 020 7253 6679
www.ourworld.compuserve.com/home-
pages/dancing_times/dthome.htm
Monthly magazine with reviews
and features about British dance.

Musical Stages

PO Box 8365, London, W14 0GL
Tel/Fax: 020 7603 2221
www.musicalstages.co.uk
Quarterly magazine with reviews
and features about British musical
theatre.

Opera Magazine

36 Black Lion Lane, W6 9BE
Tel: 020 8563 8893
Fax: 020 8563 8635
www.opera.co.uk
Monthly magazine with reviews
and features about British opera.

Opera Now

Rhinegold Publishing, 241 Shaftesbury
Avenue, WC2E 8TF
Tel: 020 7333 1700
Bi-monthly magazine with reviews
and features about British opera.

Plays & Players
Heathmill Multimedia, Northway House, 1379 High Road, N20 9LP
Tel: 020 8343 6112
Fax: 020 8343 7831
Quarterly magazine with reviews and features about British theatre.

Plays International
The Performing Arts Trust, 33A Lurline Gardens, SW11 4DD
Tel/Fax: 020 7720 1950
www.playsinternational.co.uk
Monthly magazine with reviews of British and international theatre.

Sounds Great!
PO Box 1572, Ascot, Berks, SL5 0PF
Tel: 01344 291398
Fax: 01344 621021
www.soundsgreat.co.uk
10 issues a year with listings of classical concerts and events in London and the south east.

TICKET SALES AGENTS

Box Offices

Ambassador Theatre Group
Duke Of York's Theatre St Martin's Lane, WC2N 4BG
Tel: 020 7369 1730

Delfont Mackintosh Theatres
Prince Of Wales Theatre Coventry Street W1V 8AS (Office Only)
Tel: 020 7930 9901
Fax: 020 7930 8970
www.delfont-mackintosh.com

Upstage
Tel: 020 7369 1789

Really Useful Theatres
39-45 Shaftesbury Avenue, W1D 6LA
Tel: 020 7494 5550
www.rutheatres.com
Group Sales
Tel: 020 7494 5454
Fax: 020 7494 5154
Theatre Breaks
Tel: 020 7494 537
Class Act
Tel: 020 7494 5456
Tel: 020 7494 5155
VIP
Tel: 020 7494 5451

Ticket Agencies

Albemarle
74 Mortimer Street, W1N 8HL
Tel: 020 7637 9041
Fax: 020 7631 0375
www.albemarle-london.com

Fenchurch
90-98 Shaftesbury Avenue, W1D 5EB (Office Only)
Tel: 020 7851 0300
Fax: 020 7494 0267
www.theatreticket.co.uk

Global Tickets
British Visitor Centre, 1 Regent Stree SW1Y 4XT
Tel: 020 7734 4555
Fax: 020 7734 0220
www.globaltickets.com

Lashmars
80 Duke Street, Grosvenor Square,
W1M 5DQ
Tel: 020 7493 4731
www.londontheatre.co.uk/lashmars

tkts-Official Half Price and Discount Theatre Ticket Booth
Clock Tower Building, Leicester
Square, WC2
www.tkts.co.uk

Rakes
188 Shaftesbury Ave, WC2H 8JN
4 Irving Street, WC2
31 Coventry Street, W1V 7FH
Unit 1, The Hippodrome, Cranbourn
Street, WC2 7JN
3 St Martins Court, WC2A 6GH
Tel: 020 7851 0300
www.londontheatrebookings.com

Stargreen Concert Box Office
20 Argyle Street, W1V 1AA
Tel: 020 7734 8932
www.stargreen.com

West End Theatre Bookings
343 Station Road, Harrow
Middlesex, HA1 2AA
Leicester Sq Underground, WC2
& 35 Long Acre, WC2
Tel: 020 8427 6566
www.uktickets.co.uk

Phone/Online

First Call
Seatem House, 39 Moreland Street,
EC1V 8BB (Office Only)
Tel: 0870 906 3801
www.firstcalltickets.com

Ticketmaster
46 Leicester Square, WC2H 7LR
(Office Only)
Tel: 0870 590 0123
www.ticketmaster.co.uk

Group Bookings

Groupline
22-24 Torrington Place, WC1E 7HF
(Office Only)
Tel: 020 7580 6793
www.groupline.com

The Theatregoers Club of Great Britain
Harling House, 47-51 Great Suffolk
Street, SE1 0BS
Tel: 020 7450 4040

Theatre Breaks

Bill Wright's Capital Breaks
The Pines, Woodhead Road,
Holmfirth, HD9 2SA
Tel: 01484 682255
www.londonbreaks.com

Latest Events
Total Entertainment, Juniper House,
Seager Buildings, Brookmill Road,
SE8 4JT (Office Only)
Tel: 0870 787 1787
www.latestevents.com

Radisson Edwardian
140 Bath Road, Hayes, Middlesex,
UB3 5AW (Office Only)
Tel: 0800 374411
www.radissonedwardian.com

Theatre Breaks
PO Box 1, St Albans, AL1 4ED
Tel: 01727 840244
www.theatrebreaks.com

ACT III - THE NIGHT

3.1 Where To Go
A walk through the theatre; Etiquette, Conventions & Terms explained

3.2 After The Show (or Before)
Restaurants, Wine Bars & Brasseries, Pubs, Cafés & Tea Venues, Later Entertainment

3.3 Alternatives To The Show
Other entertainment suggestions

Royal Opera House

Where To Go

If you are spending a fortune on tickets – and nowadays most producers don't give you any other option – you want to make sure you get the most out of your evening. Be certain to allow yourself plenty of time to reach the theatre, especially if you have not been there before. London theatres are spread over a much wider area than Broadway, and it's easy to take a wrong turn if you are not familiar with the territory.

Bear in mind that you will never find a parking space near the theatre, that traffic can clog up the streets delaying buses or taxis, and that the natural state for a tube train is stationary in a tunnel. On the subject of taxis, don't forget the (surely) apocryphal story of the taxi driver delivering someone late at *The Mousetrap*, whose passengers fled without giving him a tip, so he responded with a tip of his own, shouting after them "The ********* did it!".

Much better to arrive early and have time to admire the fabulous architecture – sometimes it's the best part of the evening! If you miss the start of the show you may have to wait for a suitable break before you can be seated.

There is no longer any dress code for audiences at London theatres, and Black Tie is unusual, even for first nights. It may be more egalitarian to welcome people in jeans, but it does lack a sense of style. The only recommendation therefore is that whatever you wear should not provoke a response from the attendants along the lines of: "What have you come as?"

You enter via the Foyer where you used to be welcomed by a Commissionaire or link man. I knew of one whose opening gambit was "Enter a different world". Sadly this is no longer the case, but you may get a weak smile from the manager (if it's the regular one's night off). In the Foyer you will find the Box Office – except for the London Palladium where the Box Office has a separate entrance to the left of the main doors. This dates from the time when the Palladium presented twice nightly variety with no advance booking so they had to process large crowds of people very quickly. Usually the Box Office has different windows for buying tickets and collecting prepaid ones. Sometimes the prepaid desk is on the opposite side of the Foyer to help with crowd control.

If you are collecting tickets aim to arrive in plenty of time. Five hundred people all trying to collect their tickets in the last five minutes before Curtain Up can cause delays. It also offers no opportunity for the Box Office staff to sort out any difficulties if you have booked through an agent and there is a problem. Incidentally, the start of the show is always called Curtain Up regardless of whether or not there is a curtain, and if there is one, in which direction it moves – nowadays curtains can go down as well as up. Once you have your ticket you can confirm which part of the theatre you are in. You may need to go back outside to a separate entrance if you are in the Balcony or Upper Circle. A few last vestiges of the British class system still remain.

You can then explore the building. Drury Lane has many paintings and sculptures dotted around the Front Of House – the term for the public part of the theatre. In the Royal Opera House the Grand Staircase and the Crush Bar boast huge allegorical paintings. The corridor at the rear of the Dress Circle of the Olivier Theatre at the National has a permanent exhibition about its history from 1848, which includes plans and designs for the various theatres proposed to house the company which were never built.

Because most theatres are listed Victorian buildings, toilets are not so plentiful as in modern ones. The Bars are generally open from 45 minutes before the performance starts, and some offer sandwiches, cakes and coffee as well as drinks. Only the Barbican, the National, the Royal Opera House and Shakespeare's Globe have restaurants. Bars range from the Stalls at the New Ambassadors which enjoys the intimacy of a tube train in the rush hour, to the sumptuous Grand Saloon at Dress Circle level at Drury Lane, the grandest theatre Bar in the world. It's almost worth the price of admission to enter there alone.

Star Tip: The Stalls Bar at the Palace Theatre has an adjoining picture gallery with a fascinating collection of photographs and drawings of past productions. At the Adelphi the Front Stalls Bar has a collection of material relating to the works of composer Vivian Ellis while the Side Stalls Bar features a display about performer Jessie Matthews. At the Prince of Wales the Stalls Bar has a large collection of posters from previous productions. At the Phoenix the Dress Circle Bar contains a collection of Noel Coward memorabilia.

Prince Edward Theatre

Do order your drinks for the interval in advance. It seems to be a great British tradition not to do this. I don't know why this is – guilt at having too good a time perhaps? Or the suspicion that the Bar staff will walk off into the sunset to start a new life on the proceeds of your drinks order? Theatre Bar prices are high, but not that high! Whatever the reason, most London theatregoers seem to prefer the 'no pleasure without pain' route. They wait until the interval and then jostle each other out of the way, fighting for the attention of the Bar staff, so that (all the ice having gone) they finally raise a glass of tepid liquid to their lips, just as the first bar bell rings to herald the start of Act II. Then they have to knock it back in one gulp. Take my advice – don't join in. Order in advance and watch the scrum with an air of amused superiority.

Star Tip: Some bars no longer sell wine by the glass but in $1/4$ bottles (2 glasses) so for the interval, 1 bottle with 2 glasses is perfect.

Your entertainment can begin in the foyer with the Front Of House announcements. I can assure you that if you have seen Michael Frayn's comedy *Noises Off* the truth is sometimes not too far distant. I once worked with a stage manager whose vocal technique was slightly more mannered than Maggie Smith, and I actually used to see audience members turn and look at the speaker while she was talking.

As you pass into the Auditorium (that's the bit where the seats are) remember that unlike in Broadway theatres, London programmes must be paid for. The first London playbills – literally a simple list of cast and scenes – were issued free to audiences at the Olympia Theatre in 1850. The National Theatre still gives away free cast lists today. The first programmes as we know them now were introduced at the St James's Theatre in 1869.

In the last few years the quality of material in programmes has improved considerably, and they are better value for money. Unfortunately they have succumbed to the current plague of designerism, so that the look often outranks practical use or meaning. Programmes are now likely to be in red on black, or overprinted across some complicated graphic image at a jaunty angle, in letters so small they belong in a photocopier agreement. This renders them illegible under the atmospheric lighting conditions prevailing in most auditoria. It used to be only critics who needed to bring a torch, but nowadays, unless you want to wait until you get home to find out what the play was about, it's worth taking their lead.

Programmes are only available in English, but can usually be bought in advance from the Box Office if this is not your first language and you need to do some research before the night – or don't own a torch. Give a second glance to the person selling you the programme or showing you to your seat, as many are aspiring or resting performers. On a number of occasions people have moved directly from the Auditorium to the Stage of the same theatre – but this will hopefully not happen on the night you are there. The most successful example of this was Nell Gwynne. Originally one of Mrs Mary Meggs's orange sellers in the stalls of Drury Lane, she graduated to the stage in John Dryden's *The Indian Queen* in 1665, at the age of 15. King Charles II saw her, fell in love with her, and took her as his mistress.

To help you find your seat, the numbering in most London theatres starts from low numbers on the Auditorium Right – that is as you face the stage – running to the high numbers on the Auditorium Left.

Usually you will find a small pair of binoculars attached to the rear of the seat in front of you, which are known as Opera Glasses. These can be liberated from their clamp by the insertion of an ever increasing number of coins. They usually have a warning on them that they are useless outside the theatre to deter thieves. Unfortunately there is no warning that they are pretty useless inside the theatre too.

As you settle into your seat, remember that for copyright reasons you are not allowed to take photographs, or make video or audio recordings during the performance. If you attempt to do so the attendants will ask you to stop, and the manager may ask you to surrender your equipment for the remainder of the show, and it will be returned to you minus the film or tape. Also, if you have one with you, turn off your mobile phone or pager. The climax of a recent first night was ruined by one beeping at the crucial moment. I recently heard an announcement asking people to turn phones and pagers off which continued through a huge list of electrical equipment including egg timers and hair curlers, but said that pacemakers were OK.

Talking of announcements, your heart need not necessarily sink if you hear the words "owing to the indisposition of …" During the run of Alan Bennett's play *The Lady In The Van* two actors 'portrayed' Bennett as a character in the piece. When one of them was suddenly absent due to the immanent birth of his child, the audience heard the announcement "at this performance the role of Alan Bennett will be played by Alan Bennett".

ost West End shows are run like efficient military machines with more
an competent first and second understudies on standby to cover illness
d holidays. Of course you do get the occasional Charge Of The Light
igade. I recall a flu epidemic during the original production of *Jesus
Christ Superstar* when we had great difficulty scraping together 12 apos-
s for the Last Supper. We had to resort to females from time to time,
d on one occasion ended up with 13, but I liked to think that these
cidents made for interesting theological discussions for the audience in
e interval.

here is a mystical line that runs through the theatre. It divides the
dience's area Front Of House from the performer's area Backstage.
hese two worlds meet in one place, the Fourth Wall of their respective
eas, defined by the Proscenium Arch, – the decorated frame which
rrounds the Stage opening. Usually when you take your seat it is
led with the curtain or Tabs, the most extravagant Victorian example of
hich are to be seen at Wyndhams Theatre.

usicals usually start with the overture, the magic moment when the
ouse lights dim a little and the theatrical experience takes an anticipa-
ry hold of the audience. Meanwhile backstage panic is sometimes
gendered – the equivalent of the realisation that the plane has taken
f with the baggage door still open. I recall one performance of *Me
nd My Girl* when holiday, sickness and non-arrival combined to
plete personnel to an unprecedented extent. The overture saw the
sistant choreographer resetting the dance routine in the second
mber of the show for the second leading lady and two boys instead of
ree – neither of whom had been on before.

n alarming trend on Broadway is for Musical Directors to throw away
eir batons (like cripples at an evangelist's meeting) and jig about rather
an actually conduct, sometimes for the overture, sometimes for the
hole show. Fortunately this has yet to spread to the West End, but if
ou find yourself at outbreak do complain to the manager – it's always
etter to stop an epidemic as early as possible. Incidentally, one advan-
ge of sitting in the front row is that if the show has dull patches you
n peruse the MD's reading matter over his or her shoulder.

hen the Tabs finally rise, or go 'Out' – i.e. out of the audience's sight –
t the end they fall or come 'In') the performers come on. Once there,
they move away from the audience, they are going 'Upstage', or come
wards the audience, 'Downstage'. This is because at one time all stages
d a slope or rake to improve sightlines, so the performers had to get

used to working on the side of a hill. The only remaining London theatres with a built-in rake are Drury Lane and the Haymarket. Stage Left and Stage Right are the performers left and right as they face the audience – the opposite of Auditorium Left and Auditorium Right.

Owing to the propensity of nineteenth century theatres to burn down the Iron or Safety Curtain must be lowered in the interval, to prove that it is in working order. Thus should a fire break out on stage the audience can be sealed off and protected. The performers, being professionals, are permitted by the licensing authority to be fried. At the first night of *The Lady Of Lyons* at the Shaftesbury Theatre in 1888 the Iron having been lowered could not be raised again, and after an hour the performance was abandoned, as was the entire run. In case you are wondering this was the Shaftesbury theatre which stood in Shaftesbury Avenue almost opposite the Palace (where the Fire Station is now) which was destroyed by World War II bombing. The first Iron was installed in 1800 in Drury Lane (which had previously burnt down in 1672) only to see it destroyed by fire again in 1809. Sometimes Irons are richly painted in keeping with the plasterwork of the surrounding proscenium and boxes, such as the Piccadilly, some feature cherubs as at the Haymarket, others are simply inscribed with the motto, 'For Thine Especial Safety'. The most elaborate are a reproduction of an Italian Renaissance painting at the Phoenix, and a view of the auditorium – complete with audience – at the Victoria Palace.

A further fire prevention precaution is the Drencher. When set off this creates a sheet of water across the width of the Proscenium Arch, again designed to stop fire spreading from the stage into the auditorium, which once started cannot be stopped until the entire contents of the water tank has run through. It can make a very effective finale to a production of *110 In The Shade* – a play and musical about a rainmaker. However, the control for the Iron is always located next to the control for the Drencher and there have been occasions in intervals… Well let just say it takes an awful lot of mopping up before Act II can start.

It used to be possible to order Afternoon Tea to be served in your seat the interval at matinées. An attendant would arrive with a tray containing a proper earthenware teapot, with loose tea (not teabags), a china cup and saucer, a plate of sandwiches and a slice of Dundee cake – and all for a modest sum. No longer, alas. In those days the attendants and bar staff all seemed to be female and past retirement age. I recall seeing one such lady emerge gingerly from the rear Stalls Bar at the Albery

Prince Edward Theatre

...th three trays balanced on top of each other and miss her footing. ...ccessful comedy careers have been based on less entertainment value ...an that.

...you look up to the ceiling in the Auditorium there is often a central ...me. In some theatres such as the Victoria Palace and the Shaftesbury ...is could be rolled to one side, or opened in half in the interval to ...crease ventilation on summer nights. This was particularly useful in ...e those building constructed as music halls, where drinking and ...oking were de rigeur, but it should be remembered that at one time ...theatres allowed smoking in the auditorium.

...ith a bit of luck (and the consummate skill of the practitioners), you ...lly will be transported to a different world for two and a half hours, ...d all too soon it will be Curtain Down. Again it is Curtain Down ...gardless etc. etc. etc. As you leave you may go past the Stage Door, ...here at the Palace and Prince Edward theatres you will see the inscrip- ...n: "Through this door have passed and will pass some of the greatest ...rs of the British theatre". Hopefully you will think "Tonight I was ...vileged to share time with some of them".

AFTER THE SHOW (OR BEFORE)

Eating and drinking establishments come and go at an alarming speed London, but some institutions continue forever. Here is a selection of my favourites from the long runners popular with theatre people. As always you will find the producers and stars in the Royal Box suggestions, the billed artists in the Dress Circle, and the chorus and crew in the Upper Circle.

Restaurants

Royal Box (First Class)

Café Royal Grill Room
68 Regent Street, W1
Tel:020 7437 9090
Gilt mirrors and red velvet; "the most beautiful dining room in London" – Cecil Beaton.

The Ivy
1 West Street, WC2
Tel: 020 7836 4751
London's "Sardi's" remains the ultimate fashionable theatre rendezvous.

Rules
35 Maiden Lane, WC2
Tel: 020 7 836 5314
www.rules.co.uk
Opened in 1798, it claims to be the oldest restaurant in London – game a speciality.

Savoy Hotel Grill
The Strand, WC2
Tel: 020 7836 4343
www.savoygroup.co.uk
Legendary location offering a great British menu.

Simpsons in the Strand
100 The Strand, WC2
Tel: 020 7836 9112
www.simpsons-in-the-strand.co.uk
Solid traditional British surroundings and food – roasts a speciality

Dress Circle (Club Class)

Joe Allen
13 Exeter Street, WC2
Tel: 020 7836 0651
Even more a part of the theatre scene in London than its New York cousin.

La Barca
80 Lower Marsh, SE1
Tel: 020 7928 2226
Typical traditional Italian service and menu.

Bentley's
11-15 Swallow Street, W1
Tel: 020 7734 4756
Traditional club style dining room offering outstanding fish dishes.

Bertorelli's
44A Floral Street, WC2
Tel: 020 7836 3969
www.santeonline.co.uk
Art Deco with a twist (decorative style) and Italian basics.

Brown's
82-84 St Martin's Lane, WC2
Tel: 020 7497 5050
A former courthouse with
Oxbridge style and Brideshead
ambience.

Le Café du Jardin
28 Wellington Street, WC2
Tel: 020 7836 8769
Modern Mediterranean menu in
simple elegant surroundings.

Café Pacifico
5 Langley Street, WC2
Tel: 020 7379 7728
More Mex than Tex. A lively
cantina atmosphere with modern
Mexican menu.

Chez Gerard at the Opera Terrace
45 East Terrace, Covent Garden, WC2
Tel: 020 7379 0666
www.santeonline.co.uk
Inside the conservatory or outside
on the terrace on the roof of the
old market building.

Christopher's
18 Wellington Street, WC2
Tel: 020 7240 4222
Modern American décor and grill
menu – good for steak and fish.

The Criterion
224 Piccadilly, W1
Tel: 020 7930 0488
Original Victorian Neo-Byzantine
gold and blue décor with a
modern Italian/American menu.

L'Escargot
48 Greek Street, W1
Tel: 020 7437 2679
A Soho institution that has
modernised itself of late but retains
its reputation for quality.

French House Dining Room
49 Dean Street, WC2
Tel: 020 7437 2477
Tiny restaurant with a modern
British menu above the pub
famous for its artist clientele.

Giovanni's
10 Goodwin's Court,
St Martin's Lane, WC2
Tel: 020 7240 2877
Classic Italian style food and atmo-
sphere in an ultra discreet location.

Au Jardin des Gourmets
5 Greek Street, W1
Tel: 020 7437 1816
Traditional French elegance with
modern French cuisine.

RS Hispaniola
Victoria Embankment, WC2
Tel: 020 7839 3011
A restaurant ship offering a superb
view of the Thames and a modern
Mediterranean menu.

Kettners
29 Romilly Street, W1
Tel: 020 77346112
Go upstairs for the real atmosphere
as downstairs it's just a pizza place
– there's a champagne bar if you
want to push the boat out.

Luigi's
15 Tavistock Street, WC2
Tel: 020 7240 1795
Gracious old school Italian atmosphere and food.

Manzi's
1-2 Leicester Street, WC2
Tel: 020 7734 0224
London's oldest Italian fish restaurant famous for its simple well executed dishes.

Mon Plaisir
21 Monmouth Street, WC2
Tel: 020 7836 7243
Family run French restaurant with intimate atmosphere and traditional cuisine.

Neal Street Restaurant
26 Neal Street, WC2
Tel: 020 7836 8368
décor matched with Antonio Carluccio's inventive cooking.

Orso
27 Wellington Street, WC2
Tel: 020 7240 5269
Joe Allen's more sophisticated elder brother serving a modern Italian food.

Petit Robert
3 Park Street, SW1
Tel: 020 7357 7003
Extraordinarily good French food in a seemingly ordinary setting.

Porters
17 Henrietta Street, WC2
Tel: 020 7836 6466
www.porters.uk.com
Traditional English fare – pies a speciality.

Saleri
376 Strand, WC2
Tel: 020 7836 1318
Highly theatrical décor, modern international cuisine – and a harpist.

Sarastro
126 Drury Lane, WC2
Tel: 020 7836 0101
www.sarastro-restaurant.com
Over-the-top Operatic Baroque atmosphere "the show after the show" and modern Mediterranean menu.

J Sheekey
28-32 St Martin's Court, WC2
Tel: 020 7240 2565
Famous fish restaurant which has undergone a successful makeover.

Teatro
93-107 Shaftesbury Avenue, W1
Tel: 020 7494 3040
Chic minimalist décor and moder menu have combined to create a current hot favourite.

Tiddy Dols
55 Shepherd Market, W1
Tel: 020 7499 2357
18th century Mayfair house preserving its Hogarthian atmosphere offering traditional English fayre.

Wheelers
12A Duke Street, SW1
Tel: 020 7930 2460
Narrow period townhouse of oak and stained glass serving a renowned fish menu.

Upper Circle (Economy)

Centrale
16 Moor Street, W1
Tel: 020 7437 5513
An old style Italian/Cockney café.

Ed's Easy Diner
12 Moor Street, W1
Tel: 020 7439 1955
& Trocadero Shaftesbury Avenue, W1
Tel: 020 7287 1951
American style 1950s diner with traditional menu.

Food For Thought
31 Neal Street, WC2
Tel: 020 7836 0239
Homely veggie heaven with a change of menu daily.

Gaby's Deli
30 Charing Cross Road, WC2
Tel: 020 7836 4233
London's New York style deli diner.

Jimmy's Restaurant
23 Frith Street, W1
Tel: 020 7437 9521
Old time Italian family café.

Mildred's
58 Greek Street, W1
Tel: 020 7494 1631
Friendly home cooking veggie café.

My Old Dutch
131 High Holborn, WC1
Tel: 020 7242 5200
Dutch pancake house with gigantic plates.

Pasta Brown
31-32 Bedford Street, WC2
Tel: 020 7836 7486
& 35-36 Bow Street, WC2
Tel: 020 7379 5775
Modern no nonsense pasta cafés.

Pollo
20 Old Compton Street, W1
Tel: 020 7734 5917
Simple Italian menu in substantial portions.

The Rock & Sole Plaice
47 Endell Street, WC2
Tel: 020 7836 3785
A no-frills great British fish and chip shop.

Steph's
39 Dean Street, W1
Tel: 020 7734 5976
Fun atmosphere and fun food.

The Stockpot
18 Old Compton Street, W1
Tel: 020 7287 1066
& 38 Panton Street, SW1
Tel: 020 7839 5142
Very cheap and very cheerful English grub.

Wine Bars & Brasserie

The Archduke
Concert Hall Approach,
South Bank, SE1
Tel: 020 7928 9370
Between the potted palms underneath the arches – the venue on the South Bank.

Bachanalia Wine Bar
1A Bedford Street, WC2
Tel: 020 7836 3033
www.bacchanalia.net
A Victorian basement with lots of private corners.

Le Beaujolais
Litchfield Street, WC2
Tel: 020 7836 2277
Popular, unpretentious French wine bar.

Café Boheme
13 Old Compton Street, W1
Tel: 020 7734 0263
French classic wine and food – and live jazz.

Le Café des Amis Du Vin
11-14 Hanover Place, WC2
Tel: 020 7379 3444
Classic French wine bar with a stylish modern makeover.

Conservatory Bar
15 St Giles High Street, WC2
Tel: 020 7836 8956
Surprisingly good food and drink in an unlikely setting – late music on weekends.

Cork & Bottle
44-46 Cranbourn Street, WC2
Tel: 020 7734 7807
Most Londoner's favourite – huge wine list and great food in a usually heaving basement.

Crusting Pipe
27 The Market Covent Garden, WC2
Tel: 020 7836 14156
Authentic Dickensian atmosphere often mellowed by a string quartet

Davys at St James
Crown Passage Vaults,
20 King Street, W1
Tel: 020 7839 8831
A warren of former silver vaults provides a uniquely intimate environment.

Dover Street Wine Bar
8-10 Dover Street, W1
Tel: 020 7629 9831
www.doverst.co.uk
As famous for its live jazz as its wine and food.

The Fire Station
150 Waterloo Road, SE1
Tel: 020 7620 2226
Former emergency services depot transformed into a cavernous bar.

Garrick Wine Bar
10-12 Garrick Street, WC2
Tel: 020 7240 7649
Sit upstairs and watch the comings and goings at the famous club.

Gordon's Wine Bar
(Rudyard Kipling lived here)
47 Villiers Street, WC2
Tel: 020 7930 1408
Deliciously dark and dingy cellar with open fire in winter and summer terrace.

Grape Street Wine Bar
224A Shaftesbury Avenue, WC2
Tel: 020 7240 0686
Bright modern and cheery and a good selection of wines.

Hamptons
15 Whitcomb Street, WC2
Tel: 020 7839 2823
Plain and simple with a wide choice of wines – exactly what a wine bar should be.

PJ's Grill
30 Wellington Street, WC2
Tel: 020 7240 7529
New England style service and menu.

Da Marco
417 Strand, WC2
Tel: 020 7836 0654
Narrow wood panelled rooms with an authentic Victorian air.

Randal & Aubin
16 Brewer Street, W1
020 7287 4447
Deli turned seafood/rotisserie bar.

Soho Brewing Company
41 Earlham Street, WC2
Tel: 020 7240 0606
Copper brewing vats in the ancient cellar create an unusual atmosphere and there's interesting food as well.

Tuttons
11-12 Russell Street, WC2
Tel: 020 7836 4141
Choose indoors or out on the Covent Garden Piazza.

Walkers Wine Bar
Craig's Court, 15 Whitehall, SW1
Tel: 020 7976 1961
An entire house of bars with a wide range of wines and ales.

Pubs

The Anchor
34 Park Street, SE1
Tel: 020 7407 1577
Reputedly Shakespeare's local in Bankside (and lives up to expectations of the Bard's boozer).

The Captain's Cabin
4 Norris Street, SW1
Tel: 020 7930 4767
Formerly the Cock Tavern an 18th century coaching inn.

Coach & Horses
29 Greek Street, W1
Tel: 020 7437 5920
The setting of the play *Jeffrey Bernard Is Unwell*, presided over by Norman Balon aka "the rudest landlord in London".

The Coal Hole
91 Strand, WC2
Tel: 020 7836 7503
The basement bar appears not to have changed in 100 years.

The Crown
51 New Oxford Street, WC1
Tel: 020 7836 2752
Warm welcome inside in winter and plenty of space outside under the fairy lights in summer.

De Heims
11 Macclesfield Street, W1
Tel: 020 7437 2494
Traditional Dutch hospitality – popular with stage crews.

The French House
49 Dean Street, WC2
Tel: 020 7437 2477
One of the most famous Soho locals – known for its artist clientele.

The George Inn
77 Borough High Street, SE1
Tel: 020 7407 2056
Original 17th century coaching inn – supposedly where Nicholas Nickelby departed for Dotheboys Hall.

The Hand & Racquet
48 Whitcomb Street, SW1
Tel: 020 7930 5905
The haunt of comic Tony Hancock and his writers Ray Galton and Alan Simpson who referred to it in their shows.

Kemble's Head
61 Long Acre, WC2
Tel: 020 7836 4845
Named after Philip Kemble the manager of Covent Garden and Drury Lane.

The Lamb & Flag
32 Rose Street, WC2
Tel: 020 7497 9504
Open since 1627 it claims to be central London's oldest tavern.

Lyceum Tavern
354 Strand, WC2
Tel: 020 78367155
Oak panelled rooms associated with Henry Irving.

The Nag's Head
10 James Street, WC2
Tel: 020 7836 4678
Hertfordshire ales and etchings of Covent Garden theatres – popular with Opera House staff.

Ye Old Cheshire Cheese
145 Fleet Street, EC4
Tel: 020 7353 6170
The epitome of the Victorian city pub with genuine atmosphere.

Opera Tavern
23 Catherine Street, WC2
Tel: 020 7636 7321
Traditional Victorian style – haunt of Drury Lane show cast members

Old Bank of England
194 Fleet Street, EC4
Tel: 020 7430 2255
Once the Law Courts branch of the Bank of England now spectacularly restored.

Punch & Judy
40 The Market Covent Garden, WC.
Tel: 020 7379 0923
Named in honour of Britain's first puppet show presented under St Paul's portico opposite.

Roundhouse

1 Garrick Street, WC2
Tel: 020 7836 9838
The haunt of theatregoers since 1868.

The Round Table

St Martin's Court, WC2
Tel: 020 78366436
Authentic dark wood panelled rooms – popular with show crews.

The Salisbury

St Martin's Lane, WC2
London's greatest Victorian pub and the most popular with theatrefolk – featured in the film *Travels With My Aunt*.

Sherlock Holmes

10 Northumberland Street, WC2
Tel: 020 7930 2644
Full of Holmesian memorabilia with small museum upstairs – the sign depicts Holmes on one side and Watson on the other.

Silver Cross

25-33 Whitehall, SW1
Tel: 020 7930 8350
The site of an inn since 1867 it features much Victorian memorabilia.

The Ship & Shovel

1 & 3 Craven Passage, WC2
Tel: 020 7838 1311
Two separate buildings on each side of an alleyway.

Three Greyhounds

25 Greek Street, W1
Tel: 020 7287 0754
Eclectic Soho clientele create a unique atmosphere.

Cafés & Tea Venues

Royal Box (First Class)

Brown's Hotel

Albemarle Street, W1
Tel: 020 7408 1837
Website: www.brownshotel.co.uk
Step back in time to a Victorian town house of great character.

Fortnum & Mason Soda Fountain

181 Piccadilly, W1
Tel: 020 7734 8040
Website: www.fortnumandmason.co.uk
A London original inspired by 1950s America.

The Ritz Palm Court

150 Piccadilly, W1
Tel: 020 7493 8181
Website: www.theritzhotel.co.uk
A charming room with a view across Green Park

Waldorf Hotel Palm Court

The Aldwych, WC2
Tel: 020 7836 2400
Tea among the potted palms, marble and mirrors – dances if you desire.

Dress Circle (Club Class)

Museum Street Café

47 Museum Street, WC1
Tel: 020 7405 3211
Upmarket foodie approach to teatime classics.

National Portrait Gallery Café
St Martin's Place, WC2
Tel: 020 7306 0055
Website: www.npg.org.uk
Offers views across the rooftops of
Trafalgar Square and Westminster.

Richoux
171 Piccadilly, W1
Tel: 020 7493 2204
A stylish continental coffee house.

St Martin in-the-Fields Café in the Crypt
5 St Martin's Place,
Trafalgar Square, WC2
Tel: 020 7839 4342
Website: www.stmartin-in-the-fields.org
Cream cakes in the atmospheric
brick arches beneath the famous
church.

Upper Circle (Economy)

Amalfi
29-31 Old Compton Street, W1
Tel: 020 7437 7284
Simple Italian décor and sensa-
tional Italian cakes.

Bar Italia
22 Frith Street, W1
Tel: 020 7437 4520
Preserves the '50s family run
espresso coffee bar atmosphere.

Cappucetto Patisserie
9-10 Moor Street, W1
Tel: 020 7437 9472
Homely Italian café with terrific
cakes and pastries.

Maison Bertaux
28 Greek Street, W1
Tel: 020 7437 6007
Actress Michelle Wade, who
started as a waitress and now owns
the company, stages occasional
performances upstairs.

Neal's Yard Bakery
6 Neal's Yard, WC2
Tel: 020 7836 5199
Freshly baked bread and veggie
food.

Patisserie Valerie
44 Old Compton Street, W1
Tel: 020 7437 3466
Retains its student café air despite
being packed with showbiz types –
and wonderful cakes.

Internet Cafes

EasyEverything
457-459 Strand, WC2
www.easyEverything.com
All the charm of a call centre but
lots of terminals and open 24/7.

Global Café
15 Golden Square, W1
Tel: 020 7287 2242
www.globalcafe.net
Interesting cuisine, art gallery and
events.

Webshack
15 Dean Street, W1
Tel: 020 7439 8000
www.webshack-cafe.com
Smaller quieter café.

Later Entertainment

Pizza Express
10 Dean Street, W1
Tel: 020 7437 9595
A special outlet of the franchise which features regular appearances by world class jazz musicians.

Pizza On The Park
11 Knightsbridge, SW1
Tel: 020 7235 5273
London's only remaining cabaret room presenting a repertoire of sophisticated entertainers.

Ronnie Scotts
47 Frith Street, W1
Tel: 020 7439 0747
www.ronniescotts.co.uk
Ronnie is gone but his premier jazz venue continues.

ALTERNATIVES TO THE SHOW

Comedy Store
Oxenden Street, WC2
Tel: 020 7344 4444
Britain's National Theatre of comedy – late shows on weekends.

Holland Park Theatre
Holland Park, W8
Tel: 020 7602 7856
Open air opera performances June - August.

House Of Magic
At a secret location in central London
Tel: 020 7735 3434
www.houseofmagic.co.uk
An entire enchanted house is the spectacular setting for a show of baffling illusions.

ICA
(Institute of Contemporary Arts)
The Mall, SW1
Tel: 020 7930 3647
www.ica.org.uk
Performance art at its most esoteric.

Jongleurs
49 Lavender Gardens, SW11
Bow Wharf, 221 Grove Road, E3
& Camden Lock, 211-216
Chalk Farm Road, NW1
Tel: Central booking 020 7564 2500
www.jongleurs.com
Nationwide chain of comedy clubs has the original and two other branches in London.

Kenwood Concerts
Kenwood House Hampstead Lane, NW3
Tel: Booking 020 7420 0220
www.picnicconcerts.com
Open-air classical concerts by the lake in July and August.

London Showboat
Westminster Pier, SW1
Tel: 020 7237 5134
Cabaret and dinner as you cruise down the Thames past the sights of London.

Magic Circle

12 Stephenson Way, NW1
Tel: 01322 221592
www.themagiccircle.co.uk
Regular public shows and tours at the home of British magicians.

Medieval Banquet

The Beefeater, Ivory House, St Katherine's Dock, E1
Tel: 020 7480 5353
www.medievalbanquet.com
Join Henry VIII for a medieval banquet and entertainment experience.

Murder Mystery Dinner Theatre

New Connaught Rooms,
61-63 Great Queen Street, WC2
Tel: 020 7404 4232
www.murderevents.co.uk
Solve a crime as you dine in a central London hotel.

Players'

The Arches (Off Villiers Street), WC2
Tel: 020 7839 1134
www.theplayerstheatre.co.uk
Victorian Music Hall with bar and restaurant.

Talk Of London

Parker Street, WC2
Tel: 020 7224 9000
Presents an inclusive cabaret meal and dancing package.

FREE TICKETS FOR RECORDINGS

BBC Audience Services

PO Box 3000, BBC TV Centre,
London, W12 7RJ
Tel: 020 8576 1227
Fax: 020 8576 8802
Show Information: 020 7765 5858
www.bbc.co.uk/whatson/tickets

FreemantleMedia

1 Stephen Street, W1T 1AL
Tel: 0207 691 6000
Fax: 0207 691 6100
www.gameshows.co.uk

Hat Trick Productions TV Shows

10 Livonia Street, W1V 3PH
Ticket Unit Tel: 020 7287 1598
www.hat-trick.co.uk

LWT Productions TV Shows

London Television Centre,
Upper Ground, London, SE1 9LT
Ticket Unit Tel: 020 7737 8888
LWT.Tickets@granadamedia.com

Talkback Productions TV Shows

26 Newman Street, W1P 3HB
Ticket Unit Tel: 020 7323 3777

TV Recordings

Avalon Television,
4A Exmoor Street, W10 6BD
Tel: 020 7598 5000
Fax: 020 7598 7300
www.tvrecordings.com

FINALE - THEATREGOERS LONDON

4.1 Tours
Make your own Theatreland walking tour (with map)
Conducted Walking Tours; Backstage Tours

4.2 Theatrical Calendar
Events month by month

4.3 Places Of Theatrical Interest
Museums, Exhibitions & Research Facilities, Blue Plaques, Churches, Statues & Monuments

4.4 Theatre Shops
Books, Records & Music, Memorabilia, Theatre Suppliers, Publishers & License Holders

4.5 Education
Dance Schools, Drama Schools, Music Schools, Classes & Courses

4.6 Contacts
Organisations, Producers

4.7 Bibliography

Lyric Theatre

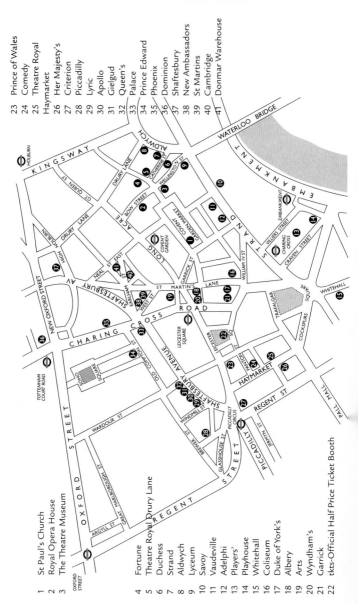

Tours

Make Your Own Theatreland Walking Tour

The tour starts and ends under the portico of **St Paul's Church** (1) in Covent Garden, where the opening scene of Shaw's *Pygmalion* – or Lerner and Lowe's *My Fair Lady* – takes place. An inscription records that Samuel Pepys saw the first Punch and Judy show in England here in 1662, hence the name of the pub in the Market building opposite. It is known as the actor's church as it contains plaques commemorating many theatrical figures, and memorial services are often held there.

As you make your way you will find that many of the streets in the Covent Garden area are named after actors and managers including Betterton, Garrick, Irving, Kean, Keeley, Kemble and Macklin.

Walk through the north aisle of the market building, passing Pollock's Toy Theatre shop on the left, to the north east corner of the piazza where there is now an entrance to **Royal Opera House** (2). The bookshop, and the café in the Floral Hall, originally the flower market, are open all day.

Exit at the front of the building in Bow Street. Opposite is another kind of theatre – Bow Street Magistrate's Court, and next door, the building where the Bow Street Runners (the predecessors of the modern police force) were based. Turn right and walk down Bow Street. On the next corner to the right you will see **The Theatre Museum** (3).

Turn left into Russell Street and on the left is **Fortune** (4).

On the right is the colonnade at the side of **Theatre Royal Drury Lane** (5). Cross over, walk back under the colonnade and turn left into Catherine Street. On the corner is a drinking fountain dedicated to Sir Augustus Harris, manager of Drury Lane in the late 19th century, who was nicknamed "Druriolanus". Just beyond is the famous portico with the royal crest.

Continue down Catherine Street and on the right is **Duchess** (6). At the bottom of the street on the left is **Strand** (7), located with typical British cunning, not in the Strand but in Aldwych.

Turn left into Aldwych. Above the door to the right of the theatre, at number 11 is a blue plaque marking the entrance to the flat where composer and performer Ivor Novello lived, and which is now a theatre producer's office. Walk past the Waldorf Hotel (or pop in for a Tea Dance) and at the other end of the block is **Aldwych** (8). Opposite and just ahead you will see Bush House, home of BBC World Service radio.

Retrace your steps to the end of Catherine Street, continue to the end of Aldwych and turn right into the Strand, as in the music hall song "Let's all go down the Strand". On your right in Wellington Street is another famous portico, that of **Lyceum** (9). In the Strand the first turning on the left is Savoy Street, off which is Savoy Hill where the BBC's – and the world's – first radio studios were located.

Continue along the Strand, and on the left in Savoy Court, the entrance to the Savoy Hotel, is **Savoy** (10). Only the box office is above ground level here as it is on a steeply sloping site – the original entrance was on the Embankment.

Almost opposite on the right is Southampton Street where on the left above the door at number 27 is a bronze plaque with a bas-relief profile commemorating where actor manager David Garrick lived. Further along the Strand on the right is **Vaudeville** (11), and **Adelphi** (12).

Continue along the Strand until you reach Charing Cross station. Turn left into Villiers Street and then right into The Arches under the station – as in the song "Underneath The Arches I dream my dreams away". Here on the left is **Players'** (13), where Sandy Wilson's show *The Boy Friend* was first presented, and which keeps the Victorian Music Hall tradition alive. Emerging from the The Arches you pass between the two halves of the Ship and Shovel pub.

At the end of the alleyway turn left into Craven Street, and at the bottom on the left is **Playhouse** (14).

Make a U-turn to the right into Northumberland Avenue, and then turn left into Great Scotland Yard, the original home of the Metropolitan Police. At the end turn right into Whitehall and on your left is **Whitehall** (15). To its left is Horse Guards Parade where yet another kind of theatre, The Changing Of The Guard, takes place.

Continue along Whitehall northwards, skirt the eastern side of Trafalgar Square, past St Martin-in-the-Fields church on the right, where free lunchtime recitals are held, into St Martin's Lane, noting the animated figure of a barrel maker above The Chandos pub on the corner. On the right is **Coliseum** (16). This is a London landmark because it is surmounted by a tower with a globe on top, whose internal lighting gives it the effect of revolving at night.

Almost opposite is **Duke of York's** (17). Further up on the left is Cecil Court, an alleyway where there are a number of theatrical ephemera shops.

Keep going and also on the left is the great genuine Victorian theatre pub The Salisbury, next door to **Albery** (18).

A little further on you come to a junction of five streets. To the right is Garrick Street, where the Garrick Club, the famous gentleman's club which has counted many actors amongst its members, is located at number 15 – a rather dowdy building on the right. Ignoring that, and with only a glance ahead to the right at Stringfellow's, take the second exit to the left, Great Newport Street and on the right is **Arts** (19).

At the end of this short street turn left into Charing Cross Road, passing on your right the Hippodrome, built to stage circus and water spectaculars but now a nightclub. On your left is **Wyndham's** (20), and further on, also on the left is **Garrick** (21).

Cross over the road and you will find an imposing statue of Sir Henry Irving, the first actor to be knighted in 1895, standing on a large plinth in a small garden backing on to the rear of the National Portrait Gallery, at the junction of Irving Street. The gallery houses portraits of many theatrical figures. Walk along Irving Street into the south side of Leicester Square and on your right is **tkts-Official half Price Ticket Booth** (22) located in the clock tower pavilion.

Skirt round the western side of Leicester Square, noting the statue of William Shakespeare, which forms the centrepiece to the fountain in the middle of the garden, and the hand prints of actors in the footpath next to the railings. Turn left into New Coventry Street. The ornamental clock on the Swiss Centre plays a glockenspiel medley with an automota display at certain hours. Continue ahead into Coventry Street. On the left is **Prince of Wales** (23).

Turn left into Oxendon Street, where The Comedy Store, the British national theatre of comedy, is on the right. At the next corner is **Comedy** (24). Turn right into Panton Street and then left into Haymarket, and on the left is the Nash portico of **Theatre Royal Haymarket** (25) with its royal crest over the entrance. Cross over the road and opposite is **Her Majesty's** (26), where there is a bronze plaque commemorating actor manager Herbert Beerbohm Tree, its builder. At the rear of the theatre is the Royal Opera Arcade, all that remains of the additions made to the earlier theatre by Nash in 1818.

Walk back up Haymarket to the top, and turn left into Piccadilly Circus. On the right is the London Pavilion, once a great music hall, where Marie Lloyd sang "the boy I love is up in the gallery", and in 1886 the first London theatre to have tip up seats, but now sadly reduced to a shopping centre. Ahead on the left is **Criterion** (27), almost opposite another London icon, the Shaftesbury Memorial – the statue popularly known as Eros. The view up Shaftesbury Avenue from here is the image that usually represents London Theatre, as Times Square does Broadway. Misplaced good taste has decreed that Piccadilly Circus can no longer compare with the neon lights of Times Square as they are now restricted to just one building.

Take the forth exit to the left Glasshouse Street, almost immediately forking right into Sherwood Street and on your right is **Piccadilly** (28).

Turn right into Denman Street at the end of which on the left in Windmill Street is the Windmill Theatre. Its motto "we never closed" – referring to the fact that it continued to play throughout World War II – was often corrupted to "we never clothed" as it presented non-stop revue, with a programme which alternated nude tableaux and comedians. Although there have been ordinary shows staged there, it has returned to its origins and is now a table dancing establishment. Turn left into Shaftesbury Avenue, and on your right is the Trocadero, another music hall now reduced to a shopping centre.

This is the heart of London's Theatreland with **Lyric** (29) and **Apollo** (30) next door to each other and **Gielgud** (31) and **Queen's** (32) forming the ends of the next block. In the buildings above and between these last two are the offices of Really Useful Theatres, London's premiere theatre chain which operates these four theatres (among others).
Continue up Shaftesbury Avenue to Cambridge Circus and on the left is **Palace** (33), another London landmark.

Turn left at the side of the theatre into Romilly Street and on the next corner on the right is the Coach & Horses, the pub that is the setting for the play Jeffrey Bernard Is Unwell, presided over by Norman Balon 'the rudest landlord in London'. Turn right into Greek Street and on the next corner on the left is **Prince Edward** (34).

Turn right into Old Compton Street and then left into Charing Cross Road, and on the right is **Phoenix** (35). Opposite is the famous Foyles bookshop, which is arguably London's largest. Continue up to St Giles Circus, passing on the right the monument to 1960s property speculation, Centre Point which remained unoccupied for 20 years. Looking left into Oxford Street, the Tottenham Arms pub is on the site of Oxford Music Hall. Ahead on the right is **Dominion** (36).

Turn right into New Oxford Street and immediately right again into St Giles High Street, passing on the right St Giles-in-the-Fields, another church which has seen many theatrical memorial services. Continue on, crossing the upper part of Shaftesbury Avenue, and on the left is **Shaftesbury** (37). Public outcry at plans to demolish it after the run of Hair was brought to an end by the ceiling falling in, organised by Save London's Theatre Campaign, led to the founding of The Theatres Trust to protect endangered theatres.

Retrace your steps to Shaftesbury Avenue, turn left and walk back towards Cambridge Circus, passing the ABC cinema on your right. This was formerly the Saville theatre, and again an outcry was caused when it was converted to twin cinemas without any notice in 1970. It was the last West End theatre to be lost to live performance.

Just before Cambridge Circus on the right is Angels the premier British costumier. Turn left into West Street almost opposite and on the left are **New Ambassadors** (38) and **St Martin's** (39). *The Mousetrap*, the world's longest running play, opened at the first and then transferred to the second. Opposite is The Ivy, the restaurant with great theatrical connections – London's equivalent to Sardi's (if such a thing could exist).

At the end of West Street turn left into Monmouth Street, pausing to see if any stars emerge from the building on the corner, which houses the actors union Equity. Walk up, passing Dress Circle, London's greatest showbiz record and bookshop on the right, to Seven Dials, where **Cambridge** (40) is on the right.

Take Earlham Street, which runs along its left side, and **Donmar Warehouse** (41), London's only "Off Broadway" theatre is on the left. At the end of Earlham Street turn right into Neal Street, passing on your right Neal Street East, a cornucopia of things oriental including Kabuki masks. Continue straight ahead, crossing Long Acre, and at the end of James Street is Covent Garden. This is where you started at **St Paul's Church** (1).

Conducted Walking Tours

These usually last about two hours and take place all year round regardless of the weather.

Facade Theatreland Walking Tour

43A Garthorne Road, SE23 1EP
Tel: 020 8699 8655
Regular tours of London's theatreland with both group and individual tours.

Ghosts Of The West End

Original London Walks,
PO Box 1708, NW6 4LW
Tel: 020 7624 3978
✍ *www.walks.com*
Visit the gaslit alleyways – plus over 100 other walks in mornings, afternoons and evenings every day.

The London Of Dickens And Shakespeare

3 Florence Road, South Croydon,
CR2 0PQ
Tel: 020 8668 5327
Southwark and Bankside on Sunday mornings plus others.

Historical Tours

The Shakespeare City Walk

5A Campsbourne Parade,
Hornsey High Street, N8 7PR
Tel: 020 8348 9022
Walk where the Bard worked and played. Walks take place on Tuesday, Thursday and Sunday mornings and afternoons.

Shakespeare Walks

Royal Shakespeare Company, Barbican Theatre, EC2Y
Tel: 01494 725186
Places of Will Power with particular reference to the current RSC season – times vary.

Sweet Love Remember'd

Shakespeare's Globe Theatre,
New Globe Walk, SE1 9DT
Tel: 020 7401 9919
Celebrates Shakespeare's birthday on 23rd April by walks starting in Westminster or Shoreditch with twelve sonneteers entertaining along a route through Tudor London to Bankside.

Theatreland Walking Tour

Society Of London Theatre,
32 Rose Street, WC2E 9ET
Tel: 020 7557 6700
Visit the West End's most historic theatres monthly on Sunday afternoons on the official tour, which includes tea and a map.

Backstage Tours

These take place at:
Barbican Centre
Drury Lane
Haymarket
London Palladium
New London
Royal National Theatre
Royal Opera House
Sadler's Wells
Shakespeare's Globe
Contact theatres for details.

Stage Doorman's Office, London Palladium

THE THEATRICAL CALENDAR

January

New Year's Day London Parade
Research House, Fraser Road, Greenford, Middlesex, UB6 7AQ
Tel: 020 8566 8586
Recorded information hotline: 0900 525 2001 (UK only)
⊰ www.londonparade.co.uk
Marching bands and floats parade around the West End.

London International Mime Festival
35 Little Russell Street, WC1A 2HH
Tel: 020 7637 5661
Fax: 020 7323 1151
⊰ www.mimefest.co.uk
Presenting visual theatre, mime, circus, puppetry and clowning from around the world.

Chinese New Year (late in the month)
Gerrard Street/Wardour Street, W1
⊰ www.chinatown-online.co.uk/pages/new_year/index.html
Chinatown celebrates with lion dancing, fire crackers and food.

Take A Date/Bring A Mate (last week)
Society Of London Theatre, 32 Rose Street WC2E 9ET
Tel: 020 7557 6700
Fax: 020 7557 6799
⊰ www.officiallondontheatre.co.uk
Special prices for young theatregoers.

February

Evening Standard Awards
Northcliffe House 2 Derry Street W8 5TT
Tel: 020 7938 6000
⊰ www.thisislondon.com
London's own theatre awards.

March

The Laurence Olivier Awards
Society Of London Theatre
⊰ www.officiallondontheatre.co.uk/olivier/main.cfm
Britain's premier theatre awards.

April

Chaucer Festival (early in the month)
Southwark Cathedral, London Bridge, SE1 9DA
Tel: 020 7229 0635
✍ www.dswark.org/cathedral
Costumed procession to the Tower of London for a medieval Fayre celebrating Chaucer's Canterbury Tales.

Shakespeare's Birthday (23rd)
Shakespeare's Globe, New Globe Walk, SE1 9DT
Tel: 20 7401 9919
✍ www.shakespeares-globe.org
Programme of celebrations.

May

May Fayre & Puppet Festival
St Paul's Church, Covent Garden, WC2E 9ED
Tel: 020 7375 0441
Celebrates Punch and Judy's anniversary.

Barbican International Theatre Event (until October)
Barbican Theatre & Pit, Silk Street, EC2Y 8BQ
Tel: 020 7638 8891
✍ www.barbican.org.uk
Presents international theatre and dance companies.

Museums & Galleries Month
Tel: 020 7233 6789
✍ www.museumsweek.org.uk
Special events at museums and galleries.

June

Spitalfields Festival
75 Brushfield Street London, E1 6AA
Tel: 020 7377 0287
Fax: 020 7247 0494
✍ www.spitalfieldsfestival.org.uk
Classical music in a striking baroque church.

London International Festival Of Theatre
19-20 Great Sutton Street, EC1V 0DR
Tel: 020 7863 8017
⊘ www.lift-info.co.uk
Presenting cutting edge theatre companies from all over the world.

City of London Festival
Bishopsgate Hall, 230 Bishopsgate. EC2M 4HW
Tel: 020 7377 0540
Fax: 020 7377 1972
⊘ www.colf.org
Presents a diverse range of art forms in splendid City buildings.

July

Almeida Opera Festival
Almeida Theatre, Almeida Street, Islington, N1 1TA
Tel: 020 7359 4404
⊘ www.almeida.co.uk
Presenting contemporary opera and music events.

The BBC Proms (to September)
Box Office, Royal Albert Hall, Kensington Gore, SW7 2AP
Tel: 020 7589 8212
⊘ www.bbc.co.uk/radio3/proms
The world's greatest classical music festival.

August

Theatrical Garden Party
St Paul's Church, Covent Garden, WC2E 9ED
Tel: 020 7375 0441
The stars come out for a traditional fete.

Kids Week (last week)
Society Of London Theatre
⊘ www.officiallondontheatre.co.uk/education/kidsweek.cfm
Children go free to West End shows with paying adults.

Notting Hill Carnival (last weekend)
Ladbrooke Grove, W10
⊘ www.nottinghillcarnival.net.uk/
Europe's biggest street festival.

London Tango Festival

September

London Open House (third weekend)
PO Box 25361, London, NW5 1GY
✎ *www.londonopenhouse.org*
Offers access to normally private buildings of architectural interest,
usually including backstage tours.

October

Dance Umbrella
20 Chancellors Street, W6 9RN
Tel: 020 8741 4040
Fax: 020 8741 7902
✎ *www.danceumbrella.co.uk*
Presenting the best of national and international contemporary dance.

Perrier Pick Of The Fringe
Duchess Theatre Offices, Catherine Street, WC2B 5LA
Tel: 020 7836 7333
Fax: 020 7836 7444
✎ *www.perrierawards.com*
Winners and nominees of the Edinburgh Festival Fringe Comedy
awards play the West End.

November

London Tango Festival
Las Estrellas, 80 Queensway, W2 3RL
Tel: 020 7221 5038
Fax: 020 7229 6339
✎ *www.tangoinlondon.com*
Classes, demonstrations and shows.

Lord Mayor's Show (third Saturday morning)
✎ *www.lordmayorsshow.org*
Marching bands and floats parade around the City of London.

December

Spitalfields Winter Festival
See Spitalfields Festival page 207
Christmas music by candlelight in a striking baroque church.

PLACES OF THEATRICAL INTEREST

Museums, Exhibitions & Research Facilities

Barbican Performing Arts & Music Library - Music Performance Research Centre
Barbican Centre, Silk Street, EC2 8DS
Tel: Library 020 7638 0672
Tel: Music Performance Research Centre 01932 860472
www.musicpreserved.org
Performing arts books, scores and recordings of live performance and interviews.

British Library - National Sound Archive
96 Euston Road, NW1 2DB
Tel: Library 020 7412 7513
Fax: Library 020 7412 7511
Tel: National Sound Archive 020 7412 7440
Fax: National Sound Archive 020 7412 7441
www.bl.uk
The Department of Manuscripts holds scripts submitted to the Lord Chamberlain's office for licensing plus playbills and theatre notices. The National Sound Archive contains recordings of performance and interviews.

Dulwich College Archives
Dulwich, SE21 7LD
Tel: 020 8299 9201
Fax: 020 8299 9245
www.dulwich.org.uk/history/archives.htm
Contain 11,000 books, diaries, account books and correspondence of its founder, the actor Edward Alleyn, and actor manager Phillip Henslowe (both contemporaries of Shakespeare) as well as manuscripts and letters of P G Wodehouse.

The Raymond Mander & Joe Mitchenson Theatre Collection
Jerwood Library of the Performing Arts, Trinity College of Music, King Charles Court, Old Royal Naval College, SE10 9JF
Tel: 020 8305 3893
Fax: 020 8305 3993
www.mander-and-mitchenson.co.uk
A cornucopia of theatrical ephemera.

Museum of London
150 London Wall, EC2V 5HN
Tel: 020 7600 3699
Fax: 020 7600 1058
www.museumoflondon.org.uk
Traces the history of London including entertainment.

National Art Library
Victoria & Albert Museum, Cromwell Road, SW7 2RL
Tel: 020 7942 2400
Fax: 020 7942 2401
www.nal.vam.ac.uk
First folios of plays by Shakespeare, Beaumont, Fletcher and Webster, exhibitions and talks.

National Portrait Gallery
St Martin's Place, WC2H OHE
Tel: 020 7306 0055
Fax: 020 7306 0056
www.npg.org.uk
The collection includes paintings, photographs and busts of many performers and writers.

Pollocks Toy Theatre Museum
1 Scala Street, W1P 1LT
Tel: 020 7636 3452
www.tao2000.net/pollocks
Original toy theatres and models on display and also on sale.

The Rose Theatre
56 Park Street, SE1 9AR
Tel: 020 7593 0026
www.rdg.ac.uk/rose
A light and sound presentation at the archeological site of Bankside's first theatre.

Shakespeare's Globe Exhibition
New Globe Walk, Bankside, SE1 9DT
Tel: 020 7902 1500
Fax: 020 7902 1515
www.shakespeares-globe.org
A comprehensive exhibition about theatre in the time of Shakespeare.

Theatre Museum
Russell Street, WC2E 7PR
Tel: 020 7943 4700
Fax: 020 7943 4777
Research Collection:
1E Tavistock Street, WC2E 7PA
Tel: Research Collection 020 7943 4727
⊛ www.theatremuseum.org
Public display of costumes, props, designs and ephemera plus unique
Research Collection of books, programmes, production photographs and
performance videos.

Westminster Central Reference Library
35 St Martin's Street, WC2H 7HN
Tel: 020 7641 4636
Comprehensive collection of theatre and performing arts books.

Westminster Music Library
160 Buckingham Palace Road, SW1W 9TR
Tel: 020 7641 4292
Comprehensive collection of scores and music books.

Churches

Highgate Cemetery
Swains Lane, Highgate, N6 6PJ
Tel: 020 8340 1834
⊛ www.highgatecemetery.co.uk
Resting place not only of Karl Marx, but of actors including Michael
Redgrave, Ralph Richardson, Patrick Wymark and Max Wall.

St Martin-in-the-Fields
5 St Martin's Place, Trafalgar Square, WC2N 4JH
Tel: 020 7839 8362
⊛ www.stmartin-in-the-fields.org
Playwright George Farquhar and Nell Gwyn are among those buried
here.

St Paul's Covent Garden
Bedford Street, WC2E 9ED
Tel: 020 7836 5221
Contains memorial plaques to many theatrical figures, some include a
quotation from their best known role.

St Paul's Cathedral
Ludgate Hill, EC4M 8AE
Tel: 020 7246 8348
www.stpauls.co.uk
Arthur Sullivan and many musicians are buried here and there is a memorial to Ivor Novello.

Southwark Cathedral
London Bridge, SE1 9DA
Tel: 020 7367 6712
www.dswark.org/cathedral
Shakespeare memorial with a reclining statue and stained glass window his brother Edmund is buried here.

Westminster Abbey
Broad Sanctuary, SW1P 3PA
Tel: 020 7222 7110
www.westminster-abbey.org
Poet's Corner and the resting place of many writers including Chaucer Sheridan, Dickens and Garrick's grave at the foot of the Shakespeare memorial.

Blue Plaques

John Logie Baird – inventor of television
22 Frith Street W1 (site of the first transmission in 1926)

J.M. Barrie –playwright, novelist and poet
100 Bayswater Road, W2

Jack Buchanan – actor, dancer and manager
44 Mount Street W1

Frances Hodgson Burnett – writer
63 Portland Place W1

Arthur Conan Doyle – writer
2 Upper Wimpole Street W1

John Dryden – poet and playwright
43 Gerrard Street W1

Edith Evans – actress
109 Ebury Street SW1

Nell Gwynne – actress
79 Pall Mall SW1

William Hazlett – essayist and theatre commentator
6 Frith Street W1

Henry Irving – actor and manager
15A Grafton Street W1

Lillie Langtry - actress
Cadogan Hotel, 22 Pont Street SW1

Charles Laughton - actor
15 Percy Street W1

Vivien Leigh - actress
54 Eaton Square SW1

Wolfgang Amadeus Mozart – composer
20 Frith Street, W1

Ivor Novello – composer and performer
11 The Aldwych WC2

Arthur Wing Pinero – playwright
115A Harley Street W1

Percy Bysshe Shelley - poet and playwright
15 Poland Street W1

Richard Brinsley Sheridan – playwright and manager
14 Saville Row W1

George Bernard Shaw – playwright
29 Fitzroy Square W1 (Virginia Woolf also lived here)
Side wall of the Lyric Theatre, Great Windmill Street W1

Oscar Wilde – writer
34 Tite St, SW3
Rear of Theatre Royal Haymarket, Suffolk Street SW1

P.G. Wodehouse - writer
17 Dunraven Street W1

Statues & Monuments

W S Gilbert – librettist
A memorial on the wall of the Embankment opposite Embankment Underground station.

Augustus Harris – manager of Drury Lane nicknamed 'Druriolanus'
A drinking fountain on the Catherine Street/Russell Street corner of the theatre.

Henry Irving – actor manager
A statue at the junction of Charing Cross Road and Irving Street WC

J M Barrie – playwright
A statue of Peter Pan in Kensington Gardens W2 on the west bank of the Long Water.

Richard D'Oyly Carte – impresario who presented Gilbert and Sulliv operas. A sundial in Embankment Gardens WC2 at the exit to Cartin Lane.

David Garrick – actor manager
A bronze plaque with a bas-relief profile at 27 Southampton Street WC2.

William Shakespeare – playwright
A statue forming the centre of a fountain in Leicester Square WC2.

Arthur Sullivan – composer
A bust above a figure representing music in mourning in Embankmen Gardens WC2 on the corner of Savoy Place.

Herbert Beerbohm Tree – actor manager
A bronze plaque on Her Majesty's theatre which he built.

Oscar Wilde – playwright
'A Conversation With Oscar Wilde' seat incorporating a bust in Adelai Street WC2.

HENRY IRVING
ACTOR

BORN 1838 DIED 1905 KNIGHT LITT D DUBLIN D LITT
CAMBRIDGE LL D GLASGOW ERECTED BY ENGLISH
ACTORS AND ACTRESSES AND BY OTHERS
CONNECTED WITH THE THEATRE IN THIS COUNTRY

THEATRE SHOPS

Books

Foyles
113-119 Charing Cross Road,
WC2H 0EB
Tel: 020 7440 3232
Fax: 020 7434 1574
www.foyles.co.uk

French's Theatre Book Shop
52 Fitzroy Street, W1P 6JR
Tel: 020 7387 9373
Fax: 020 7387 2161
www.samuelfrench-london.co.uk

Offstage Theatre Bookshop
37 Chalk Farm Road, NW1 8AJ
Tel: 020 7485 4996
Fax: 020 7916 8046
New and second-hand books.

Royal National Theatre Bookshop
Upper Ground, SE1 9PX
Tel: 020 7452 3456

Theatre Museum Shop
Russell Street, WC2E 7PR
Tel: 020 7943 4750

Records & Music

Argent Zwemmer Printed Music
20 Denmark Street, WC2 H 8NA
Tel: 020 7379 3384
Fax: 020 7379 3398

Boosey & Hawkes
295 Regent Street, W1R 7YA
Tel: 020 7291 7255
www.boosey.com

Chappell of Bond Street
(also instruments and publishers)
50 New Bond Street, W1V 9HA
Tel: 020 7491 2777
www.chappellofbondstreet.co.uk

Dress Circle (also books)
57-59 Monmouth Street, Upper St
Martin's Lane, WC2H 9DG
Tel: 020 7240 2227
Fax: 020 7379 8540
www.dresscircle.co.uk p

First Night Records
2 Fitzroy Mews, W1P 5QD
Tel: 020 7383 7767
Fax: 020 7383 3020
www.first-night-records.com

Music Discount Centre Opera Shop
33 St Martin's Lane, WC2N 4ER
Tel/Fax: 020 7240 0270

Rare Discs
18 Bloomsbury Street, WC1B 3QA
Tel: 020 7580 3516

Royal Opera House Shop
Covent Garden, WC2E 9DD
Tel: 020 7212 9331
Fax: 020 7240 0141

Travis & Emery
17 Cecil Court, WC2N 4EZ
Tel: 020 7240 2129
Fax: 020 7497 0790

Memorabilia

David Drummond Pleasures Of Past Times
11 Cecil Court, WC2N 4EZ
Tel: 020 7836 1142
Victorian posters, post cards and books.

Pollocks Toy Theatres
Covent Garden Market, WC2E 8HA
Tel: 020 7379 7866
Victorian model theatres.

Stage Door Prints
9 Cecil Court, WC2N 4EZ
Tel: 020 7240 1683
Fax: 020 7379 5598
Books, prints and posters.

The Witchball
2 Cecil Court, WC2N 4HE
Tel/Fax: 020 7836 2922
Prints, posters and programmes.

Vintage Magazine Shop
39 Brewer Street, W1R
Tel: 020 7439 8525
& 55 Charing Cross Road, WC2
Tel: 020 7494 4064
www.vinmag.com

Theatre Suppliers

Costume

Academy Costumes
50 Rushworth Street, SE1 0RB
Tel: 020 7928 6278
Fax: 020 7928 6287
www.academycostumes.co.uk

Angels
119 Shaftesbury Avenue, WC2H 8AE
Tel: 020 7836 5678
Fax: 020 7240 9527
www.fancydress.com

Cosprop
26-28 Rochester Place, NW1 9JR
Tel: 020 7485 6731
Fax: 020 7485 5942
www.cosprop.co.uk

Dancewear & Shoes

Anello & Davide
47 Beauchamp Place, SW3 1NX
Tel: 020 7225 2468
Fax: 020 7225 2111

Dancia International
187 Drury Lane, WC2B 5QD
Tel/Fax: 020 7831 9483
www.dancia.co.uk

Freed of London
94 St Martin's Lane, WC2N 4AT
Tel: 020 7240 0432
Fax: 020 7240 3061
www.freedoflondon.com

Gamba
3 Garrick Street, WC2E 9AR
Tel: 020 7437 0704
Fax: 020 7497 0754

Porselli
9 West Street, WC2H 9NE
Tel: 020 7836 2862
Fax: 020 7836 6171

Flying

Flying By Foy
*Unit 4 Borehamwood Enterprise
Centre, Theobald Street,
Borehamwood, Herts, WD6 4RQ
Tel: 020 8236 0234
Fax: 020 8236 0235
www.flyingbyfoy.co.uk*

Kirby's AFX
*8 Greenford Avenue, W7 3QP
Tel/Fax: 020 8723 8552
www.kirbysflying.co.uk*

Make-Up & Wigs

Banbury Postiche
*Little Bourton House, Southam Road,
Banbury, Oxfordshire, OX16 1SR
Tel: 01295 757402
Fax: 01295 757401
www.wigsuk.com*

Charles H Fox
*22 Tavistock Street, WC2E 7PY
Tel: 0870 2000 369
Fax: 0870 2001 369
www.charlesfox.co.uk*

Wig Specialities
*173 Seymour Place, W1H 5TP
Tel: 020 7262 6565
Fax: 020 7723 1566*

Musical Instruments

Ray Man
*54 Chalk Farm Road, NW1 8AN
Tel: 020 7692 6261
Fax: 020 7692 5765
www.raymaneasternmusic.co.uk*

Macari's (guitars and electric)
*92 Charing Cross Road, WC2H 0JA
Tel: 020 7836 2856
Fax: 020 7379 8762*

Paxman (brass)
*Linton House, 164 Union Street, SE1
0LH
Tel: 020 7620 2077
Fax: 020 7620 1688*

Rose Morris
*11 Denmark Street, WC2H 8LS
Tel: 020 7836 0991
Fax: 020 7240 9874
www.rose-morris.co.uk*

Jacques Samuel Pianos
*142 Edgware Road, W2 2DZ
Tel: 020 7723 8818
Fax: 020 7224 8692
www.jspianos.com*

Magic

Davenports
*Units 19-20 Charing Cross
Concourse,
5 Adelaide Street, WC2N 4HZ
Tel: 020 7836 0408
Fax: 020 7379 8828*

Props & Furniture

A + M Hire
*The Royals, Victoria Road, NW10
6ND
Tel: 020 8233 1500
Fax: 020 8233 1550
www.amhire.com*

Bapty 2000 (weapons)
Witley Works, Witley Gardens,
Norwood Green, Middlesex,
UB2 4ES
Tel: 020 8574 7700
Fax: 020 8571 5700

Camden Furniture Hire
55 Chase Road, NW10 6LU
Tel: 020 8961 6161
Fax: 020 8961 6162
www.camdenfurniture.co.uk/

Peter Evans Studios (props)
1 Frederick Street, Luton,
Bedfordshire, LU2 7QW
Tel: 01582 725730
Fax: 01582 481329

Newman Hire
16 The Vale, Acton, W3 7SB
Tel: 020 8743 0741
Fax: 020 8749 3513

Shaolin Way (martial arts)
10 Little Newport Street, WC2H 7JJ
Tel: 020 7734 6391
Fax: 020 7287 6548

Studio & TV Hire
(props and furniture)
3 Aerial Way, Wood Lane, W12 7SL
Tel: 020 8749 3445
Fax: 020 8740 9662

Scenic Supplies

Flint Hire & Supply
(paints and ironmongery)
Queens Row, SE17 2PX
Tel: 020 7703 9786
Fax: 020 7708 4189
www.flints.co.uk

Harlequin (dance floors)
Bankside House, Vale Road, Tonbridge,
Kent, TN9 1SJ
Tel: 01732 367666
Fax: 01732 367755
www.harlequinfloors.co.uk

Rex Howard Drapes
Acton Park Industrial Estate,
Eastman Road, The Vale, Acton
W3 7QS
Tel: 020 8740 5881
Fax: 020 8740 5994

Robert Knight
Top Of The Bill House, Queens Row,
SE17 2PX
Tel: 020 7277 1704
Fax: 020 7277 1722

Modelbox
(Computer Aided Design)
20 Merton Industrial Park, Jubilee
Way, SW19 3WL
Tel: 020 8254 4720
Fax: 020 8254 4721
www.modelbox.co.uk/

Mick Tomlin Drapes
109 Folly Road, Mildenhall, Suffolk,
IP28 7BT
Tel: 01638 713408
Fax: 01638 711077

Publishers & License Holders

Music Sales
8 Frith Street, W1V 5TZ
Tel: 020 7434 0066
Fax: 020 7439 2848

Musicscope
95 White Lion Street, N1 9PF
Tel: 020 7278 1133
Fax: 020 7278 4442

Warner Chappell Music
Griffin House,
161 Hammersmith Road, W6 8BS
Tel: 020 8563 5800
Fax: 020 8563 5801

Josef Weinberger
12 Mortimer Street, W1N 7RB
Tel: 020 7580 2827
Fax: 020 7436 9616
www.josef-weinberger.co.uk

EDUCATION

Dance Schools

Central School of Ballet
10 Herbal Hill, Clerkenwell Road,
EC1R 5EG
Tel: 020 7837 6332
Fax: 020 7833 5571
www.centralschoolofballet.co.uk

**London Contemporary
Dance School**
The Place, 17 Duke's Road,
WC1H 9PY
Tel: 020 7387 0152
Fax: 020 7387 3976
www.theplace.org.uk

London Studio Centre
42-50 York Way, N1 9AB
Tel: 020 7837 7741
Fax: 020 7837 3248
www.london-studio-centre.co.uk

Royal Academy of Dance
36 Battersea Square, SW11 3RA
Tel: 020 7223 0091
Fax: 020 7924 3129
www.rad.org.uk

Royal Ballet School
155 Talgarth Road, W14 9DE
Tel: 020 8748 6335
Fax: 020 8563 0649
www.royal-ballet-school.org.uk

Urdang Academy
20-22 Shelton Street, WC2H 9JJ
Tel: 020 7836 5709
Fax: 020 7836 7010

Drama Schools

**Academy of Live and
Recorded Arts**
Royal Victoria Patriotic Building,
Fitzhugh Grove, Trinity Road, SW18
Tel: 020 8870 6475
Fax: 020 8875 0789
www.alra.demon.co.uk

**Central School of Speech
and Drama**
Embassy Theatre, Eton Avenue, NW3
Tel: 020 7722 8183
Fax: 020 7722 4132
www.cssd.ac.uk
In addition to full-time training
offers evening, weekend, summer
and short courses.

Drama Centre London
176 Prince of Wales Road, NW5
Tel: 020 7267 1177
Fax: 020 7485 7129
www.dcl.drama.ac.uk

Guildhall School of Music and Drama
Silk Street, EC2Y 8DT
Tel: 020 7382 7192
Fax: 020 7256 9438
www.gsmd.ac.uk

LAMDA - London Academy of Music and Dramatic Art
Tower House, 226 Cromwell Road, SW5 0SR
Tel: 020 7373 9883
Fax: 020 7370 4739
www.lamda.org.uk

Mountview Academy of Theatre Arts
104 Crouch Hill, N4 9EA
Tel: 020 8340 5885
Fax: 020 8348 1727
www.mountview.ac.uk

RADA - Royal Academy of Dramatic Art
62-64 Gower Street, WC1E 6ED
Tel: 020 7636 7076
Fax: 020 7323 3865
www.rada.org
In addition to full-time training offers evening, weekend, summer and short courses.

Webber Douglas Academy of Dramatic Art
30 Clareville Street, SW7 5AP
Tel: 020 7370 4154
Fax: 020 7373 5639

Music Schools

Royal Academy of Music
Marylebone Road, NW1 5HT
Tel: 020 7873 7373
www.ram.ac.uk

Royal College of Music
Prince Consort Road, SW7 2BS
Tel: 020 7589 3643
Fax: 020 7589 7740
www.rcm.ac.uk

Trinity College of Music
King Charles Court, Old Royal Naval College, SE10 9JF
Tel: 020 8305 3888
Fax: 020 8305 3999
www.tcm.ac.uk

Classes & Courses

The Actor's Centre
1A Tower Street, WC2H 9NP
Tel: 020 7240 3940
Fax: 020 7242 0234

Circus Space
Coronet Street, N1 6HD
Tel: 020 7729 9922
Fax: 020 7729 9422
www.thecircusspace.com

The City Lit (The City Literary Institute)
16 Stukeley Street (off Drury Lane), WC2B 5LJ
Tel: 020 7242 9872
Fax: 020 7405 3347
Information line: 020 7831 7831
www.citylit.ac.uk

Goldsmiths College
Lewisham Way, SE14 6NW
Tel: 020 7919 7276
www.gold.ac.uk

Morley College
61 Westminster Bridge Rd, SE1 7HT
Tel: 020 7450 9232
www.morleycollege.ac.uk

Shakespeare's Globe Education Programme
21 New Globe Walk, SE1 9DT
Tel: 020 7902 1433
Fax: 020 7902 1401
www.shakespeares-globe.org
Staged readings, lectures, courses and workshops

Dance Studios

Dance Works
16 Balderton Street, W1V 1TF
Tel: 020 7629 6183
Fax: 020 7499 9087
www.danceworks.co.uk

Pineapple Dance Centre
7 Langley Street, WC2H 9JA
Tel: 020 7836 4004
Fax: 020 7836 0803
www.pineapple.uk.com

Contacts

Organisations

Arts Council of England
14 Great Peter Street, SW1P 3NQ
Tel: 020 7333 0100
Fax: 020 7973 6590
www.artscouncil.org.uk

Artsline
54 Charlton Street, NW1 1HS
Tel: 020 7388 2227
Fax: 020 7383 2653
www.artsline.org.uk

British Music Hall Society
82 Fernlea Road, SW12 9RW
Tel: 020 8673 2175

Cats Kids Club
New London Theatre, Drury Lane, WC2B 5PW
Tel: 020 7242 9802
www.reallyuseful.com/cats

The Cinema Theatre Association
Flat 1, 128 Gloucester Terrace, W2 6HP
www.cinema-theatre.org.uk
Visits to purpose built picture houses

Department for Culture, Media and Sport
2 Cockspur Street, SW1Y 5DH
Tel: 020 7211 6000
www.heritage.gov.uk

Equity
Guild House, Upper St Martin's Lane, WC2H 9EG
Tel: 020 7379 6000
www.equity.org.uk
The British actors union.

Frank Matcham Society
Flat 9, Hardwick Gardens, Hardwick Mount, Buxton, SK17 6PR
Tel: 01298 26656

Fringe Theatre Network
The Finborough Theatre, 118 Finborough Road, SW10 9ED
Tel: 020 7565 4040
Fax: 020 7835 1853
www.fringetheatre.org.uk

Haymarket Masterclasses
Theatre Royal Haymarket, SW1Y 4HT
Tel: 020 7389 9660
Fax: 020 7389 9698
www.trh.co.uk

The Irving Society
69 Harcourt Street, Newark on Trent,
Nottinghamshire, NG24 1RG
Tel: 01636 702801

Kids Theatre Club In
The West End
Theatre Museum, 1E Tavistock Street,
WC2E 7PA
Tel: 020 7943 4806
www.officiallondontheatre.co.uk/education/kidsweek.cfm#theatreclub

The Leisure Pass Group
(The London Pass)
PO Box 2337, W1A 5WE
Tel: 01664 500107
www.londonpass.com

The Mousetrap Foundation
15 New Row, WC2N 4LD
Tel: 020 7836 4388
Fax: 020 7836 4399
www.mousetrap.org.uk

Musician's Union
60-64 Clapham Road, SW9 0JJ
Tel: 020 7582 5566
Fax: 020 7582 9805
www.musicians-union.org.uk

National Campaign for The Arts
Pegasus House, 37-43 Sackville
Street, W1S 3EH
Tel: 020 7333 0375
Fax: 020 7333 0660
www.artscampaign.org.uk

National Council for Drama
Training
5 Tavistock Place, WC1H 9SS
Tel: 020 7387 3650
Fax: 020 7383 3060
www.ncdt.co.uk

National Disability Arts Forum
Mea House, Ellison Place,
Newcastle upon Tyne, NE1 8XS
Tel: 0191 261 1628
www.ndaf.org

Radar
Unit 12 City Forum,
250 City Road, EC1V 8AF
Tel: 020 7250 3222
www.radar.org.uk

Save London's Theatres
Campaign
Guild House, Upper St Martin's
Lane, WC2H 9EG
Tel: 020 7379 6000

Shape Ticket Scheme
London Voluntary Sector
Resource Centre,
356 Holloway Road, N7 6PA
Tel: 020 7700 8138

ShowPairs
PO Box 3841, London, SW1V 2XE
Information line: 020 7976 5887
www.show-pairs.co.uk
Available to companies only (not
individuals) in London and the
home counties.

ShowSavers
7600 The Quorum,
Oxford Business Park, OX4 2JZ
Tel: 01865 785000
Fax: 08705 441144
www.theatrenet.com/showsavers

SPIT – Signed Performances
in Theatre
PO Box 6028, London SW1P 3XF
Tel: 0161 773 1715
www.spit.org.uk

The Society for Theatre Research
Theatre Museum, 1E Tavistock Street,
WC2E 7PA
Tel: 020 7943 4700

Society of London Theatre
32 Rose Street, WC2E 9ET
Tel: 020 7557 6700
www.officiallondontheatre.co.uk

STAR – Society of Ticket Agents and Retailers
PO Box 43, London, WC2H 7LD
Tel: 0870 603 9011
www.s-t-a-r.org.uk

Stagetext
75 Canfield Gardens, NW6 3EA
Tel: 020 7372 1246
www.stagetext.co.uk

Theatre Investment Fund
32 Rose Street, WC2E 9ET
Tel: 020 7557 6737

The Theatres Trust
22 Charing Cross Road,
WC2H 0HR
Tel: 020 7836 8591
Fax: 020 7836 3302

Tripscope
The Courtyard, Evelyn Road,
W4 5JL
Tel: 020 8994 9294

Vocaleyes
189 Wardour Street, W1V 3FA
Tel: 020 7734 6053
Fax: 020 7734 8868
Booking line: 0870 902 0002
www.vocaleyes.co.uk

Writers Guild of Great Britain
430 Edgware Road, W2 1EH
Tel: 020 7723 8074
Fax: 020 7706 2413

Producers

Michael Codron
Aldwych Theatre Offices, Aldwich,
WC2B 4DF
Tel: 020 7240 8291
Fax: 020 7240 8467

Robert Fox
6 Beauchamp Place, SW3 1NG
Tel: 020 7584 6855
Fax: 020 7225 1638

Bill Kenwright
106 Harrow Road,
Off Howley Place, W2 1RR
Tel: 020 7446 6200
Fax: 020 7446 6222
www.kenwright.com

Andrew Lloyd Webber
(Really Useful Group)
22 Tower Street, W1V 5FD
Tel: 020 7240 0880
Fax: 020 7240 1204
www.reallyuseful.com

Cameron Mackintosh
1 Bedford Square, WC1B 3RA
Tel: 020 7637 8866
Fax: 020 7436 2683

Duncan Weldon
Suite 4, Waldorf Chambers,
11 Aldwych, WC2B 4DA
Tel: 020 7343 8800
Fax: 020 7343 8801

BIBLIOGRAPHY

The Great Theatres of London
Ronald Bergan, Prion, London, 1990

Britain in Old Photographs: Theatrical London
Patricia Dee Berry, Alan Sutton Publishing, Stroud, 1995

The Guinness Book of Theatre Facts & Feats
Michael Billington, Guinness Superlatives, London, 1982

The British Theatre
Alec Clunes, Cassell, London, 1964

The Theatres Trust Guide to British Theatres 1750-1950
John Earle & Michael Sell, A&C Black, London, 2000

The Streets of London – A dictionary of the names and their origins
Sheila Fairfield, Macmillan, London, 1983

Victorian & Edwardian Theatres
Victor Glasstone, Thames & Hudson, London, 1975

Rebuilding Shakespeare's Globe
Andrew Gurr & Ornell, Weidenfeld & Nicolson, London, 1989

London Theatres and Music Halls 1850-1950
Diana Howard, Library Association, London, 1970

Theatre and Playhouse
Richard and Helen Leacroft, Methuen, London, 1984

The Lost Theatres of London
Raymond Mander & Joe Mitchenson, Rupert Hart-Davis, London, 1968

The Theatres of London
Raymond Mander & Joe Mitchenson, New English Library, London, 1975

Empires, Hippodromes & Palaces
Jack Read, The Alderman Press, London, 1985

London Theatre From The Globe To The National
James Roose-Evans, Phaidon, Oxford, 1977

Frank Matcham – Theatre Architect
Brian Walker, Blackstaff Press, Belfast, 1980

The Oberon Glossary of Theatrical Terms (Theatre Jargon Explained)
Colin Winslow, Oberon Books, London, 1991

London Theatre Walks
Jim D Young & John Miller, Applause, New York, 1998

Directories

British Performing Arts Yearbook
Rhinegold Publishing,
241 Shaftesbury Avenue, WC2H 8EH
Tel: 020 7333 1720
Fax: 020 7333 1769
Website: www.rhinegold.co.uk

British Theatre Directory (annual)
Richmond House Publishing,
3 Richmond Buildings, London, W1V 5AE
Tel: 020 7437 9556
Fax: 020 7287 3463

Contacts (annual)
The Spotlight, 7 Leicester Place, WC2H 7RJ
Tel: 020 7437 7631
Fax: 020 7437 5881

McGillivray's Theatre Guide (biennial)
David McGillivray, Rebecca Books, London, 1996.

PLAYOUT – THE CONCLUSION

5.1 Be An Angel
How to become an investor.

5.2 Financial Tables
Production Budget, Weekly Running Costs, Recoupment Schedule

BE AN ANGEL

Theatre breeds an enthusiasm in its aficionados which, while expressing itself in a rather more reserved manner, is no less fervent than that of football supporters – and as we know the total of admissions to theatres each year is higher than that of football matches. Here is some information about how you can satiate that ardour by becoming part of the theatre, rather than just being a spectator.

People who invest in theatre productions are called Angels. This is probably because, like guardian angels, quite often there's not much return on your investment, except the knowledge that you have contributed to the greater well being of mankind. But it does give you the opportunity to become involved, and like all hobbies, it can be worth it for that alone.

Let's start with the drawbacks – remember that the curtain can go down as well as up. Of every five West End shows produced, three are flops, one breaks even, and one makes a profit. A sobering thought, but better odds than the National Lottery and a lot more fun to play.

So how does it work? When a producer decides to put on a show, he makes sure he does the one thing that marks him out as a professional – he doesn't use his own money. Having found the Property (a script he wants to produce) and bought the rights of, say, *Harry Potter – The Musical*, the producer starts by putting together a Production Budget. This is an estimate of the cost of finding and rehearsing the creative team, cast and orchestra; designing and making the scenery, costumes and props; installing them all in a theatre; and marketing the end product.

He will then decide on the Capitalisation of the project – that is the Production Budget and a Contingency Fund to sustain the show until it is on its feet. He will then go on to work out the Weekly Running Costs – the cost of hiring the theatre; the cast, orchestra and crew wages; equipment hire; creative team royalties; and continuing marketing.

Based on all this information he will produce a Recoupment Schedule showing how many weeks it will take to recover the Capitalisation at varying levels of business. Producers aim to put together a package that can recover its costs at 75% business in 39 weeks.

He then sets about raising the Capitalisation. An Investment Proposal will be issued containing the financial information referred to above, together with details and background of the cast and creative team who will realise the show. In addition, if the show is a new musical, there may be Backers Auditions. These are informal gatherings designed to encourage prospective investors to part with their money, when the director outlines the story, and some of the songs are performed.

If the Capitalisation is, say, £700,000, the producer offers perhaps 700 Units in the show at £1000 each. So if you invest £1000 you own 1/700 of it. You can generally take as many Units as you wish. If raising the money proves difficult 1/2 (half) or even 1/4 (quarter) Units may be offered.

Assuming the show is a worthwhile Property, is well put together, and enough people come to see it, each week the Net Box Office Takings, less the Weekly Running Costs, will provide a Profit. You will receive 1/700 of this Profit until Recoupment – the point at which your investment has been paid back in full.

After Recoupment the Producer takes 40% of this Profit for his insight in finding the material and expertise in guiding its production; and you continue to receive 1/700 of the remaining 60% of the Profit for as long as the run continues – in the case of *The Phantom Of The Opera* probably for ever.

If on the other hand the show is a disaster and folds, then not only are the remaining physical assets worth nothing, but the producer has to pay people to remove them from the theatre and throw them away. So you get nothing.

If financial return is your main concern, you should consult a financial advisor or put your money in a building society. The point of investing in theatre is for the fringe benefits. You will normally at least receive a pair of free tickets to the First Night and an invitation to the bash afterwards. There you can rub shoulders with the stars of your show, and hangers-on who nobody recognises, but who the publicist maintains will guarantee media coverage. If you are really lucky, the back of your head will be visible (though blurred) in the background of photographs in various colour magazines for weeks afterwards.

Depending on the producer and the show, there could be a variety of other perks. You may be invited to special promotional presentations before opening night and to birthday and other parties after. You may have access to House Seats, so you can buy tickets even though the show is sold out. You may receive a goodie bag of free merchandise, or be able to buy items at a discount. At the very least your heart will swell with pride when you pass the theatre or see any reference to your show in the media.

If you are interested in becoming an angel you can contact the Society Of London Theatre and join the potential investors list, to whom their members can circulate Investment Proposals if they wish. The more established producers (with presumably a more reliable track record) will have a waiting list of people wishing to become investors, but as costs continue to escalate all producers continually need new investors.

You could also search the internet for information on projects seeking backing which have websites. You will find online Investment Proposals as mentioned above.

If you are of a truly charitable nature you could consider a gift or bequest to the Theatre Investment Fund. This is a registered charity whose aim is to ensure the long-term health of the commercial theatre by encouraging new producers and investing in their talents. The TIF not only puts money into productions, but gives advice and support as well. Contributions to the Fund help finance commercial productions all over the country.

FINANCIAL TABLES

"The Show" – Production Budget

Pre-production Costs
Option, Advances, Casting, Administration,
Marketing, Reading & Workshop,
Provincial Theatre Deposit ---- *44,000.00*

Rehearsal Costs
Company, Orchestra, Staff Salaries, NI &
Touring Allowance, Room Hire, Rehearsal
Parts, Transportation, Petty Cash ---- *47,590.12*

Fees
Director, Designers, Choreographer,
Arranger, Marketing & PR Reps,
Photographer, Production Manager/Carpenter ---- *38,800.00*

Physical Production Costs
Set Construction, Costumes, Wigs, Props,
Lighting, Sound, Orchestrations ---- *199,000.00*

Provincial Costs
Cast, Orchestra Staff Salaries, Touring
Allowance, NI & Holiday Pay, Lighting &
Sound Hire, Orchestral Management ---- *65,307.76*

Professional Services
Accountancy, Insurance, Legal,
General Management ---- *17,050.00*

Advertising And Promotion
Marketing, Publicity, Advertising, Printing,
Distribution, Display ---- *125,000.00*

West End Costs - Pre-Opening
One Week's Rehearsal Salaries & NI,
Get In & Fit Up, Overtime ---- *36,044.18*

PRE-OPENNG PRODUCTION COSTS ---- **572,797.06**
Less estimated provincial take (plus deposit) ---- *(40,00.00)*

**TOTAL PHYSICAL PRODUCTION
COSTS TO 1ST NIGHT** ---- **532,792.00**

CASHFLOW FUNDS (Incl Escrow Accounts)
Deposits, Bonds, Hires, VAT,
Contingency & Running Losses ---- **166,709.60**

TOTAL CAPITALISATION ---- **699,501.66**

"The Show" – Estimated Weekly Running Costs

Salaries
Company, Orchestra, Staff NI & Holiday Pay ---- *18,950.50*

Fees
General & Orchestral Management, Marketing
& PR Reps, Accountancy, Fixed Royalties ---- *3,260.00*

Additional Running Costs
Insurance, Advertising, Hires,
Maintenance, Sundries, Reserve ---- *9,750.00*

FIXED WEEKLY COSTS ---- **31,960.50**

CASH CAPACITY – 1100 seats average £16.00 **105,600.00**
(average 7.5 performances, less discounts & VAT)

Rent & Contra against 15% of gross ---- *15,000.00*

BREAKEVEN FIGURE (Excluding Royalties) ---- **46,960.50**

Break + Royalties (Pre Recoupment - 10%) ---- *51,656.55*
Break + Royalties (Post Recoupment - 16%) ---- *54,474.18*

"The Show" - Recoupment Schedule - 1100 Seater Theatre

CAPACITY	NET BOX OFFICE	RENT & CONTRA	WEEKLY COSTS	ROYALTIES	TOTAL COSTS	PROFIT	WEEKS TO RECOUP
45%	47,520.00	15,000.00	31,960.50	4,752.00	51,712.50	(4,192.50)	
50%	52,800.00	15,000.00	31,960.50	5,280.00	52,240.50	559.50	
55%	58,080.00	15,000.00	31,960.50	5,808.00	52,786.50	5,311.50	132
60%	63,360.00	17,004.00	31,960.50	6,336.00	55,300.50	8,059.50	87
75%	79,200.00	19,380.00	31,960.50	7,920.00	59,260.50	19,939.50	35
80%	84,480.00	20,172.00	31,960.50	8,448.00	60,580.50	23,899.50	29
90%	95,040.00	21,756.00	31,960.50	9,504.00	63,220.50	31,819.50	22
100%	105,600.00	23,340.00	31,960.50	10,560.00	65,860.50	39,739.50	18

Typical Theatres: Aldwych, Cambridge, Phoenix, Piccadilly, Savoy, Strand

PLEASE NOTE:

Post Recoupment the above figures will reflect an increase in salaries, creative royalties and theatre rental. A creative royalty waiver operates below break figure (not shown).

Photography Credits

p.II Open Air, Regents Park © Alastair Muir / p.2 Duchess Theatre © English Heritage, p.7 Her Majestys Theatre © English Heritage / p.15 Prince Edward Theatre © English Heritage, p.17 London Palladium © English Heritage / p.18 London Palladium © English Heritage / p.21 Duchess © English Heritage / p.33 Apollo Victoria © English Heritage / p.39 Barbican © English Heritage / p.45 English National Opera © Tim Flach / p.56 BOSTON MARRIAGE by David Mamet at Donmar Warehouse. Pictured: Zoe Wanamaker (Anna), Anna Chancellor (Claire) © John Haynes / p.59 Royal Drury Lane © English Heritage / p.62 Duchess © English Heritage / p.77 Duchess © English Heritage / p.81 Lion King, Javine Hylton (Nala), Roger Wright (Simba).
© Disney/Photography by Catherine Ashmore / p.86 Royal National Theatre © Gautier Deblonde / Open Air, Regents Park © Alastair Muir / p.113 Prince Edward © Claudia Bierwirth / p.123 Royal Opera © Rob Moore / p.127 Sadler's Wells © Morley von Sternberg / p.129 Sadler's Wells © Morley von Sternberg / p. 137 Shakespeare's Globe © Donald Cooper / p.150 Drury Lane © English Heritage / p.155 Lyric Theatre © English Heritage / p.161 Her Majestys Theatre © English Heritage / p.162 Queens Theatre © English Heritage / p.165 Queens Theatre © English Heritage / p.171 Make-up Workshop © The Theatre Museum / p.176 The Royal Opera House © Rob Moore / p.179 Prince Edward © English Heritage / p.182 Prince Edward © English Heritage / p. 185 Prince Edward © English Heritage / p. 197 Lyric © English Heritage / p. 205 London Palladium © English Heritage / p. 209 © London Tango Festival / p. 229 Apollo © English Heritage

Order Form

The following titles are also available from Metro Publications:

Gay & Lesbian London	£7.99	
A Taste of London	£6.99	
The London Market Guide	£5.99	
The Guide to Cookery Courses	£7.99	
Museums & Galleries of London	£8.99	
Bargain Hunters' London	£6.99	
The London Theatre Guide	£7.99	

Please tick the boxes representing the books you would like to order and fill in your details below:

Name: _____

Address: _____

_____

Send your order along with a cheque made payable to
Metro Publications to the address below.
Metro Publications,
PO Box 6336, London N1 6PY
email: metro@dircon.co.uk
www.metropublications.com

You can also get our guides via a customer order line on
020 8533 0922 (Visa/Mastercard/Switch)
Open: 9am-6pm; Mon-Fri

Postage is free, please allow 14 days for delivery.

Gay & Lesbian London
Author: Graham Parker
£7.99, 260pp, 40 b/w photos, 4 Maps
ISBN 1-902910-09-5

Gay & Lesbian London includes reviews of all the social clubs, political organizations, health services, restaurants and night clubs to help gay men and woman enjoy the Capital. The book is essential for exploring the Capital's gay scene.

Taste of London
Author: Jenny Linford
£6.99, 144pp, 42 b/w photos
ISBN 0-9522914-7-9

A Taste of London contains over 80 cosmopolitan recipes, many of them recommended by Londoners of diverse ethnic origin and using all the ingredients to be found in the Capital, from dried porcini mushrooms to root ginger and lemon grass. The book also contains a glossary of cooking ingredients.

The London Market Guide
2nd edition
Authors: Andrew Kershman & Ally Ireson
£5.99, 192pp, 40 b/w photos,
80 Maps
ISBN 1-902910-04-4

The London Market Guide contains all the essential information needed to explore London's 7 street markets including maps, photos, travel information, consumer tips, over 90 cafés and full contact details for those wanting to get a stall.

The Guide to Cookery Courses
Cooking & Wine Schools, Courses &
Holidays Throughout The British Isles &
Further Afield (2nd edition)
Author: Eric Treuille
£7.99, 210pp, 10 b/w photos
ISBN 1-902910-05-2

The Guide to Cookery Courses has been
updated and expanded to provide a
comprehensive listing of the cookery and
wine courses in the British Isles and
further afield.

Museums & Galleries of London
2nd edition
Author: Abigail Willis
£8.99, 288pp, 60 b/w photos,
3 Area Maps & 8 Floor plans
ISBN 1-9029-10-079

This is the first guide to combine detailed
reviews of all the museums and galleries
of London with listings of the city's
commercial galleries, archives and details
of London's many art degree shows

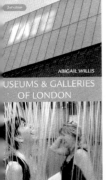

Bargain Hunters' London
2nd edition
Author: Andrew Kershman
£6.99, 288pp, 60 b/w photos,
11 Area Maps
ISBN 1-9029-10-06-0

A comprehensive guide to finding
bargains in London, including the best
charity shops, auctions, designer sales,
dress agencies, second-hand bookshops,
factory outlets, independent designers and
manufacturers and much more.

The London Theatre Guide
Author: Richard Andrews
£7.99, 288pp, 50 b/w photos,
2 Area Maps
ISBN 1 902910 08 7

This is a complete reference work about the theatres of London. It will not only answer questions a first time visitor would ask, but will also surprise the regular theatregoer with useful and interesting information.